BOLO PACHA

Also by Shelby F. Westbrook:

Tuskegee Airmen 1941-45 Publisher: Tuskegee Airmen Inc.

The Battles of the United States Colored Troops: 1863-1865. Study Guide.

BOLO PACHA

A Forgotten Story About Men & Women Who Made History in WWI

By Shelby Foster Westbrook

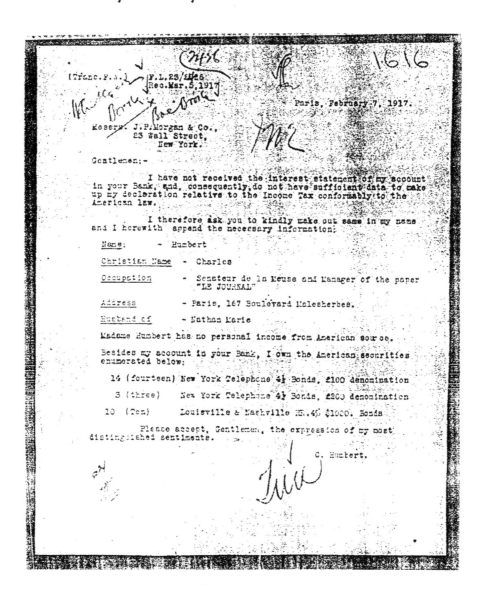

Order this book online at www.trafford.com
or email orders@trafford.com

Most Trafford titles are also available at major online book retailers.

Printed in Victoria, BC, Canada.

ISBN: 978-1-4269-2175-9 (soft)

Library of Congress Control Number: 2009913009

*Our mission is to efficiently provide the world's finest, most comprehensive book publishing service, enabling every author to experience
success. To find out how to publish your book, your way, and have it available worldwide, visit us online at www.trafford.com*

Trafford rev. 1/18/2010

 www.trafford.com

North America & international
toll-free: 1 888 232 4444 (USA & Canada)
phone: 250 383 6864 ♦ fax: 812 355 4082

Contents

Introduction

Propaganda was first used on a large scale as a military weapon during World War I, and it was a powerful weapon indeed for all of the countries involved in this conflict. This is the story of one man, Paul Marie Bolo, who was a central figure in a plot to assume control of French newspapers in order to influence the course of events in Germany's favor.

The Germans had used propaganda for many years in their colonies and in other countries where they had large investments. During the Franco-Prussian War of 1870, the French knew that Germany had used propaganda to influence the Belgians to help them obtain military information on the location of defense points, so that the German army met little resistance on its march to Paris. This was a humiliating event to the French, for they had to pay 15 billion francs to have the Germans withdraw. They also lost Alsace-Lorraine and had to endure the crowning of King Wilhelm II of Prussia as the Emperor of Germany in the Hall of Mirrors in the Palace of Versailles in 1871.

A profound change occurred in Germany's foreign policy with the resignation of Chancellor Otto Von Bismark in 1890. The German Emperor Wilhelm II was now free to rule the country without the old chancellor interfering with his authority. Count George Leo Von Caprivi, the former chief of the German Admiral, was appointed the new chancellor. Because he was beholden to Wilhelm, he could not reign in the monarch like Bismark.

Germany was determined to become a world leader on par with France and England, and Chancellor Caprivi convinced Wilhelm that Germany's future depended on the development of its industries in the world trade markets. Furthermore, a strong military was deemed necessary to protect Germany's economic progress from England and particularly France, which desired retribution for its 1870 defeat in the Franco-Prussian War. It started compulsory military service for a period of two years, causing the size of the Army to increase proportionally with the growth of the population.

Germany tripled its commercial fleet to where it was second only to England in gross tonnage, and began creating new products for world trade. To help move those goods throughout the world, representatives were dispatched to different countries to ensure that German goods were acceptable and competitive. During 1900 to 1914, Germany was exporting 100,000 men a year along with its industrial goods.

France and England had acquired large colonial areas before Germany was unified. Wilhelm was determined to make Germany a world power as well and sought expansion throughout the

Balkans to Turkey in the south. The Emperor made a trip to Constantinople to form an alliance with the Sultan of Turkey, who was at odds with England over the British occupation of Egypt. In 1899, Germany purchased from Spain the islands of Caroline, Pelew and Marianne in the Pacific. They also acquired several Samoan islands from the U.S., shoring up its foothold in the Pacific Ocean as well as Africa.

By the time World War I began in 1914, Germany was well prepared for its conflict with France. The Germans used the same tactics they employed in the Franco-Prussian War. German Secret Service operators were already established in Belgium and could furnish information to the military on the best routes to take to avoid Belgian armed forces.

The Germans were even better prepared this time since they had established a bureau for espionage and another for propaganda. The fastest route from Germany to Paris lies through Belgium, and there were more than 8,000 German agents working in Brussels, Ostend and Boulogne under Major Steinhauer, who was headquartered in the small town of Wesel in Germany. It was estimated that in the first 18 months of the war, Germany spent more than $360 million on spy operations in 18 different countries. Using informants, Germany was able to put 700,000 troops in Brussels and put them up as they advanced through the countryside.

France was rather hapless when it came to espionage. The entire staff of its Deuxieme Bureau, France's military intelligence agency at the time, was arrested by the Germans in Belgium. The French never rebuilt that bureau, and for the remainder of the war, relied on information furnished by the British. England's Scotland Yard hampered Germany's efforts to set up in that country by rounding up 14,000 Germans and Austrians during the first few weeks of the war to prevent them from becoming a problem. In Switzerland, there were so many spies and counter spies it had the appearance of a comic opera. The French arrested several hundred suspects trying to cross their border with Switzerland.

It is difficult to separate the spy from the propagandist. Both have the same purpose – to defeat the enemy. The Germans were the first to use movies to protect their ideas and extol the "humaneness" of their desire to end the conflict – of course, on their own terms. There were more than 80,000 Germans in Spain when the war started, and they became agents for distributing propaganda in France and Italy. Mexico became the center for the North and South American efforts; Berlin provided funds to operate 23 newspapers there at an estimated cost of $50,000 a month.

Into this scene stepped Paul Marie Bolo, a Frenchman of limited means and morality, but great ambition, who would play a behind-the-scenes role in Germany's insatiable quest for power through propaganda.

- - S. F. W.

Chapter 1

The Shooting

Paris   15 March 1914

The office staff of *The Figaro* had finished their work for the day, and the next day's edition was ready for printing. Gaston Calmette, the editor and owner of *The Figaro*, was meeting with a friend, Paul Bourget. After the meeting was over, the two of them prepared to depart his office.

The hall porter paid little attention to the woman approaching him, her quiet demeanor and modest attire gave him no reason for alarm. She gave him a small envelope to deliver to the editor Gaston Calmette. When Calmette received the card in the envelope, he was both surprised and uneasy, for he knew the name but not the person. Showing the card to Paul Bourget, he asked, "What will I do? It is a lady, I must receive her." The porter was showing the lady to the editor's office as Bourget was leaving. She wore a dark dress and was utterly calm and composed as she entered the office.

The editor had just removed his coat and turned to greet his visitor. As he turned, she fired the first shot, hitting him in the chest. As he fell, she fired four more shots and Calmette crumpled to the floor. After the fifth shot, the porter seized the woman's arms and held her fast. Bourget, with other staff members, rushed into the editor's office to aid the victim, however, there was nothing they could do. Four bullets from the small automatic had found their mark; one bullet passed near his heart. The doctors called were unable to save Calmette.

The police were summoned and the assailant was arrested. The mood of the office staff went from that of stunned disbelief to one of rage when told that the assailant was Henrietta Caillaux, the wife of Joseph Caillaux.

Calmette, as managing editor of *The Figaro*, was directing a scathing attack on the policies of Caillaux, the present Minister of Finance in the French government. The news of Calmette's murder brought forth a plethora of charges against Caillaux, who had once served as Prime Minister and on two other occasions as Finance Minister. It was Mme. Caillaux, however, who was indicted for murder, not her husband.

But even her closest friends were unable to account for her actions. She expressed indignation at *The Figaro*'s attack on her husband, however, she made no threats against anyone

1

at the paper. Her friends recalled her saying, "My husband should take legal proceedings against Gaston Calmette and claim damages for the publication of a private letter without the consent either of the writer or the recipient."

As the tragic events were unfolding at the office of *The Figaro*, M. Caillaux was conducting the affairs of the Ministry of Finance and was informed by a telephone call from the Chief of Police as to the shooting, as well as the location and personal condition of his wife. He left at once to go to her.

The French President Raymond Poincare and the members of the Cabinet were to have dined that evening at the Italian Embassy, however, they declined to attend after learning of the tragedy. Caillaux no doubt knew that political considerations would call for his resignation, but the welfare of his wife was now his primary concern. Caillaux secured the services of Maitre Labori, the famous defender in the Dreyfus Affair, to undertake her defense on the understanding that he will allow no reflections upon the reputation of Calmette. Labori defended Alfred Dreyfus, a French Jewish artillery officer who was tried and convicted in 1894 on charges of treason amid charges of anti-Semitism. His conviction was overturned in 1906.

Consul Labori had an interview with his client in the prison where she was confined and she was remorseful about her part in causing the death of Calmette. "I only intended to scare him," she said, "but after the first shot, I lost all control. It was a moment of madness." Her impassive manner in describing the event was similar to the cool, calm attitude shown as she fired the weapon.

Even in death, Gaston Calmette proved to be a figure of controversy. His funeral was the catalyst for civil disorder. The storm of wind and rain did little to calm the crowds. The services were held at the Church of St. Francois de Sales in the Rue Ampere, and in attendance were numerous members of literary and theatrical societies, as well as an unusually large number of politicians. The chief mourner was Calmette's brother, a chief inspector in the Army Medical Service. Sarah Bernhardt, the famous actress, was among those in attendance. The church services ended at 1:00 p.m. and the crowd started for the cemetery, which was located at the end of the Avenue de Clichy.

The police, expecting trouble, requested that the graveside services be brief. Several thousand people made up the procession to the cemetery. Many of them were violently opposed to the policies of Joseph Caillaux and intended to create disorder at the end of the funeral services. The city officials were prepared and had members of the mounted Republican Guards, the Municipal Guards and members of the Army Infantry positioned at intervals along the route to keep violence to a minimum.

The Trial

Paris   20 July 1914

The trial of Madame Caillaux for shooting Gaston Calmette, editor of the newspaper *The Figaro* and her husband's political enemy, begins before the Seine Assizes. The Court of Assizes hears cases involving murder and other serious crimes. The charge against her is one of premeditated murder, based on her actions on the day of the murder. In a letter to her husband on the day of the crime she wrote:

My Dearly Beloved Husband,

When this morning I told you of my interview with Judge Monier, who informed me that we had in France no law to protect us against calumnies of the press, you said to me that one of these [days] you would smash the face of the ignoble Calmette. I understood that your decision was irrevocable. My mind was then made up. It is I who do justice. Forgive me, but my patience is at an end. I love you and embrace you from the depths of my heart.

Your Henriette

After writing the letter, the accused went to a gun shop where she purchased the weapon. She requested and received instructions on the proper operation of the automatic. From the gun shop, she proceeded to an employment agency to hire a cook. The manager of the employment agency recalls nothing unusual in her manner or disposition.

As the public sat mesmerized by the forthcoming revelations of scandal, the politicians were busy fantasizing about the revelation of what were sure to be some embarrassing policy decisions made by the radical Socialists, the party of Joseph Caillaux. The governments of Great Britain and Germany were also aware that some of the facts could affect their mutual interests.

The people of Europe, in general, were oblivious to the seething unrest and mistrust between the major powers of the continent. Germany, Austria-Hungary and Italy had formed the Triple Alliance, while Great Britain, France and Russia joined in what was called the Triple Entente. The greatest catastrophe in the history of mankind was already on the move. Few could see it, and no one could stop it. The major attention of the public was now on the trial which had just begun.

The accused was transferred from the prison of St. Lazare to the Conciergerie, the famous prison attached to the Palais de Justice. One might have expected such a royally-named courtroom to radiate a quiet ambiance. This room, however, was rectangular in shape with faded dark blue wallpaper, a dirty molded ceiling, and somber woodcarvings – hardly fitting as the chief seat of justice for a great power.

At one end of the room on a raised platform was the judge's bench. In front of the bench, in a semi-circle, were seated the counsel for the defense, as well as counsel representing the Calmette family. There were so many journalists in the room, that there was only a small space left for the general public. The presiding judge M. Albanel, the public prosecutor M. Herbeaux and the court officials entered the room dressed in scarlet robes faced in black.

The first business of the court, selecting and swearing in of the jurors, was done with few objections. The jurors accepted were a good cross-section of the middle-class Parisians. As Judge Albanel was addressing instructions to the jurors, the prisoner was escorted into the chamber by two deputies.

The bright light from the large windows reflected the pallor of her complexion, and the redness of her eyes indicated a person under emotional distress. Her attire also appears to be designed to sway the jurors; she wore a black coat and skirt with white Baptiste collar, and a black waterproof satin hat with a large black feather that contrasted sharply with her ash blonde hair. Observers said her hands, swathed in black gloves and clutching a white handkerchief, were never at rest.

As the charges were being read describing the details of the crime, her eyes were constantly moving from the judge, the jury and to her husband sitting there in the front of the bench. The charges were voluntary homicide with premeditation on the person of Gaston Calmette.

On this hot and humid July day, a courtroom filled to capacity, the stage was set for one of the most memorable trials in French history. After the names of the witnesses were called, and made part of the court record, Madame Caillaux was called to answer the charges brought against her.

The accused rose to answer the charges and what followed was a surprise to all in the court. Her remarks were a narrative of the events of her life that were instrumental in provoking her to take the actions on that fateful day. This is the story of her life:

"I was brought up like all the young girls of my time. I never went to a boarding school and never left my parents until the day of my marriage at the age of 19 to Leo Claretie. Our characters were not in harmony and disputes soon arose. Several times I wanted my freedom, but refrained from divorce proceedings on account of my two daughters. For their sake I waited. Finally I obtained my divorce in 1908, an in 1911 I married Joseph Caillaux, who was then Prime Minister. In this marriage I found the greatest happiness. I had all, I have all. If we had not been poisoned by Calumny I should have everything to make me happy. I have a husband who returns a hundredfold the affections I have for him. I have a daughter who is the joy of our household. We had a brilliant fortune, but this fortune is not the abominable wealth which gossip had given us, but is that which we have both received from inheritance. Unhappily, slander and scandal and calumny soon entered our home. We had hardly been married when we heard the Mme. Gueydan, Caillaux's first wife, had photographs of some letters with which she wished to exact vengeance for our marriage.

"At the same time, on this slander infamous rumors were spread about my husband. All Paris knows that it was said of my husband that he was ill, that he was going mad, that he had been guilty of all sorts of extravagant antics in public. Everywhere I went, ironic smiles greeted me. I knew the people were laughing at me. I knew that I was a little ridiculous.

"Abominable rumors of ill-gotten wealth were also in circulation. My husband was said to have made a fortune on the Berlin Stock Exchange during the Moroccan crisis. He was accused of having sold the Congo to the German emperor, and the whole of Paris knew the story of the $3,000 tiara he gave me as a wedding present, paid for by the German emperor. Everywhere I went I heard horrible things said about my husband. In the gallery (senate) of the chamber when my husband rose to speak, shouts of 'Congo Caillaux, Congo Caillaux, go to Berlin!' were raised, and I had to go away in shame. These rumors spread everywhere; my friends, my tradesmen, my servants told me of them. When the Barthou Ministry fell my husband was asked to take office. I knew that the income tax *would again be discussed, and that it was that which excited people against him. I was very frightened and did not wish him to become Minister again; I told him that it would turn to sadness for him. Alas! I did not see how.*

"The Figaro campaign began. It was implacable from the start. It was personal and not political. In 95 days there were no less than 138 articles or caricatures in which my husband was attacked always of having used dishonorable means of achieving personal aims. Could one more clearly accuse a man of being not only a traitor to his country, but a thief as well?

"My husband was described as a disgrace to France. There were other slanders in which the names of the King of England and the King of Spain were mentioned. Finally, Gaston Calmette, in view of the failure of this campaign, became exasperated. In The Figaro on March 10 he wrote that the decisive moment was at hand and that no means, however contrary to taste and custom, would now be neglected. On March 13, the famous 'Tonjo' letter appeared in its columns." [This letter was one of three letters that Joseph Caillaux had written to his present wife, prior to his separation and divorce from Madame Gueydan, his first wife.]

"My husband was so afraid for my sake that we agreed to give each other up. He feared that my life might be attempted and I left France secretly for Florence, Italy. There I received a telegram informing me that the letters had been destroyed, after a promise had been given that no copies existed. Shortly after my marriage to Caillaux, we heard that copies of the letters were in existence. The letters were affectionate, they were written in the language which any well-brought man might use in writing a lady. He told me other difficulties which prevented him breaking off his marriage with Mme. Gueydan, but what was likely to be most interesting to The Figaro was that he discussed the political reasons which made it inadvisable for him to seek divorce six months before the general election. He drew a picture of the psychology of the average voter, and it would have been interesting to placard these letters on all the walls of France on the eve of the last general elections. These political matters were mingled with intimate concerns. On March 14, we heard that The Figaro was going to publish these two letters and there was every reason to fear his threat, for in The Figaro Calmette spoke of the sorrows of Mme. Gueydan, of the letters and of the papers which she had destroyed. When you think that for three years we had always had the perpetual menace of this publication handing over our heads, and that two days before we had been warned from all sides that the letters would appear on March 17, you can realize that I was convinced of the sincerity of the threat and terribly concerned when I thought of my responsibility in the matter.

"It was difficult for the publisher of The Figaro to argue that the 'Tonjo' letter was not a brutal invasion of the private life of my husband. Had not Calmette himself written after its publication, 'It is therefore a very intimate and private letter which established the felony of Caillaux'?

"When my husband said that since there was no legal means of putting an end to the Calmette campaign, he would smash his face. I want to say that by saying he would smash the face of the man who preparing to attack my honor, was only doing his duty ant that

it restored my spirits a little. I felt that I had my natural protector. If my husband had said, 'There is nothing to be done; resign yourself,' I should have thought him a coward and despised him.

"My God, my God! If you knew how I suffered that day! My good, kind husband was going to commit a crime and for my sake. I thought of killing myself and then I saw that even my suicide would be used to attack him. I would have nearly given my life to have the assurance that the letters would not be published."

[The prisoner broke down completely when asked to describe the crime scene.]

"When I decided to go to The Figaro a voice seemed to say to me, 'Take a revolver with you!' These pistols are terrible things: they go off by themselves. How could it be thought that she had fired with intention of killing. You must reason a little, she appealed to the jury that the murder could only have produced a greater scandal than that which we desired to stifle.

"I lost my head when I found myself in the presence of the man who had done us so much harm, who had ruined our lives for 13 months. It was in trying to avoid a catastrophe that I committed this act, irreparable for the unhappy victim, irreparable for my husband, my daughter and myself."

Madame Caillaux concluded her long statement by declaring, "I regret from the depths of my heart the great sorrow I have caused. I declare that I would rather anything had been published than to have been the cause of what has happened."

* * * * * *

July 22 was the third day of the trial, and also the third week since Archduke Francis Ferdinand of Austria was assassinated in Sarajevo by Serbian nationalists. An event that threatens the peace of Europe was being overshadowed by the French fascination for scandal.

Two documents found on the body of Calmette when he was shot were considered of such importance that they were forwarded to the office of President Poincare. The documents were then given to the Minister of Foreign Affairs for evaluation. The prosecutor informed the court that these documents were "alleged copies of documents which do not exist and have never existed, and that therefore they could not be used to damage in any way the honor or patriotism of M. Caillaux."

On the witness stand today was Joseph Caillaux, and like his wife, his evidence was more in the form of a speech. The courtroom was crowded and the heat was almost stifling as many in the courtroom were using fans to fight the discomfort.

Without taking the oath, M. Caillaux gave an account of his life starting with his first wife and the events leading up to the death of Gaston Calmette. Some of the letters written by him to his present wife were sent while he was still married to his first wife, Mme. Gueydan. The major part of his disclosures was, in fact, an attempt on his part to counter all the adverse criticism created by his policies as Prime Minister.

Maitre Chenu, counsel for the Calmette family, expressed admiration for the clever way that Caillaux had turned a criminal trial into a political one. "M. Caillaux will be able to leave the court with a certificate of national loyalty based upon documents known only to himself." He concluded by saying, "The court should try the real question before it – whether or not Madame Caillaux assassinated Gaston Calmette."

On the fourth day of the trial, Mme. Gueydan, the dark-haired, dark-eyed former wife of Caillaux took her seat on the witness stand. She remembered removing some letters from her husband's desk, however, she was unaware that copies had been made and she maintained that those letters contained nothing political or anything of public interest.

It seemed unlikely that letters between an adulterer and his mistress, written three years ago, would be the reason for someone to commit murder to prevent their disclosure. At the time they were written, Caillaux was Minister of Finance, and France and Germany were at odds over the control of territories and their influence in central Africa and in Morocco.

Then Mme. Gueydan surprised all in the courtroom by entrusting all of the documents in question to counsel Labori. Then she went on a scathing denunciation of the court, the defendant and her former husband. "Gutters of scandal have been emptied to throw at me. I am astonished at all the pity which seems to be lavished upon the intruder who wormed her way into my hearth, who stole my husband from me and that there has not been a single word of sympathy for the faithful wife whom this woman has made her victim. It has been said that Mme. Caillaux committed a crime because photographed letters were in circulation, and that these photographs should not have existed thanks to a bargain between my husband and myself. That is a lie."

Called as a witness, Barthou addressed the defendant: "I have the most sincere respect for your situation, but Madame, I have so far scarcely heard the prosecution say a word against you. You are defended by friends whose devotion and courage I admire. By a husband who is a living adaptation of talent. You have said that I had not worth of pity. I have had it for my lifelong friend Gaston Calmette. You have spoken of his children. They are the friends of my children. Gaston Calmette is dead, and now an attempt is being made to transform him, the victim, into an accused against who are brought not definite accusations, but insinuations. You must understand that my pity and my commiseration were for the children who lost their father and toward the man who has been assassinated."

There were also several newspapers that supported Mme. Caillaux, the *Depiche de Versailles* and the *Bonnet Rouge*, to name just two.

* * * * * *

By the fourth day of the trial, July 24, Serbia and Austria were in dispute over control of Bosnia-Herzegovina. Austria sent a harsh ultimatum to Serbia demanding that Austrian officials take part in the trial of the Serbian that assassinated the Archduke Francis Ferdinand and his wife in Sarajevo. The threat of a major conflict in the Balkans had altered the relationship among all the major powers.

The Caillaux trial was starting to be overshadowed by the drums of war. President Poincare was on a state visit to Russia aboard the battleship France. The gravity of the situation forced Poincare to cancel the trip and return to France immediately.

The Verdict

Paris   28 July 1914

The last two days of the trial were spent on the question of the financial wealth of both Caillaux and also Gaston Calmette.

The presiding judge announced that the court would not sit on Sunday. Monday and Tuesday would be devoted to the closing arguments of the counsel and very likely the jury would receive the case by Tuesday.

The 48-hour time limit placed on the ultimatum to Serbia was near. The French Foreign Office was in night sessions and a large force of police prevented crowds from street riots. There was strong opposition against France becoming involved in a war.

The question was, however, was Germany going to intervene and support Austria or would she ease the tension?

The Serbians, realizing the impending disaster, granted to Austria every demand except one. On that one they offered the matter to mediation or arbitration. On July 28, Austria declared war on Serbia. On that same day, the Caillaux case went to the jury. The question was whether Mme. Caillaux was guilty of murder; secondly, whether murder was premeditated. The jury returned after an hour of deliberation with a verdict of not guilty.

* * * * * *

At the outbreak of the war, Caillaux was 54 years of age, too old for combat duty. However, he was given a commission and the duty of Paymaster-General of the Army. He alienated the people of that department and so was relieved of that position and sent on a mission to Brazil.

He was to examine the purchase of South American supplies and the propagandist methods used by the Germans in those countries. During his term as Prime Minister, French investors had lost large sums in the railroad of Brazil. He contacted an official of the Brazilian Railroads, Farquhar, and discussed the value of the railroad industry.

At a dinner given by Farquhar, the guests included the American Ambassador and a Count James Minotto, who was the representative of the Guaranty Trust Bank of New York. Minotto became a confidant of Caillaux and was able to glean information that was useful to him, for unknown to Caillaux, Minotto was a German agent. The information he obtained from Caillaux was passed to Count Luxburg, the German minister at Buenos Aires. Luxburg in turn sent cables to the German ambassador in Washington, Count Johann Heinrich Bernstorff. Bernstorff was born in London while his father was the German Envoy to England. In 1908, Wilhelm II picked Bernstorff as the Ambassador to the United States where he remained until 1917.

The Caillauxs returned to France in April 1915. However, they found that the public, and some of their former associates as well, avoided them. They began to make new friends among those who were opposed to the war, and some were involved in events that bordered on treason. M. Caillaux began to conceive plans for a peace treaty with Germany at the expense of

Great Britain; he thought that France had suffered enough. The press accused him of seeking a German victory by pursuing a policy of "Defeatism."

The hostility that greeted the Caillauxs whenever they went out in Paris made them decide to move to Vichy, but the harassment there was even worse. On one occasion they were chased by a mob and had to take refuge in the prefecture of police.

Mme. Caillaux no longer felt safe in France, so in November 1916, the Caillauxs set up residence in Italy, first in Florence and then in Rome. They felt at home among the Italians, who were also promoting peace overtures to Germany.

Chapter 2

The Protesters

As the threat of war engrossed the attention of most people in Paris, the verdict of the Caillaux trial enraged many others. Germany was better prepared for war, and many blamed the Radical Socialists Party and its leader, Joseph Caillaux, for having opposed the cabinet's efforts to increase the nation's military.

The French, in many ways, were no match for Germany. In the 10 years before the war, the population of France grew by 300,000, while the population of Germany increased by more than 8 million. On July 27, Sir Edward Grey of the British Foreign Office, with the support of President Poincare, proposed a four-power meeting to Baron Von Schoen, the German ambassador to France, to maintain the peace of Europe. On July 28, Austria declared war on Serbia and on Aug. 4, Germany invaded Belgium. Great Britain and France were both at war with Germany.

A nation at war relies on its patriots to come to its defense, however, a war brings out that other segment of the nation. They are the protestors, the profiteers and the propagandists.

The people of France had more than their share of the latter, though they were as yet unaware of it.

A large force of police prevented crowds from gathering at many of the press bulletin boards where telegrams were posted. At Le Matin, the crowd began to chant *A Bas La Guerre* (Down with war!) and when the police tried to clear the street, they fought them with fists and walking sticks. Jean Jaures, another member of the Socialist Party who with Caillaux had opposed the conscription laws, was shot and killed as he sat in a café. The Caillauxs were also targets of the street crowds, and were afraid to go out in public.

Martial law was declared and street protests grew more peaceful, but still foreign tourists in Paris were frantically seeking passage out of the country. Some foreigners involved in the street disorders, such as Leon Trotsky, were deported.

The first passenger liner to reach New York after war was declared, the Philadelphia, had passengers sleeping on the decks, wealthy men and women with no funds or checkbooks, using jewelry and other valuables to pay for their passage. On shipboard there was neither class nor social distinctions, there was only the desire for the safe shores of the United States.

The advance of the German army was halted at the Marne River, only 30 miles from Paris. The mere thought of seeing German troops in the streets of Paris made patriots out of the protestors and they now rallied to support their government.

The Profiteers

There are those who protest to promote a cause or an idea, however, the profiteer's main impulse is to obtain wealth, regardless of the plight of the winners or the losers.

The German army had stretched its supply lines to the extreme, and now had to withdraw, less they be cut off by the French army. The French army was only strong enough to force a retreat so the combatants both dug in for a long engagement.

As the state of siege began at the front lines, a select few behind the lines began to emerge in positions they could never attain in normal times.

One such was Paul Marie Bolo, born in Marseilles in 1867, the son of a solicitor, the grandson of a notary. In his early twenties, he was a dentist in Marseilles, then a colonial grocer and a lobster merchant in his quest for greater things. None of these efforts were rewarding enough so in 1892 Bolo, as many others had done, decided to seek his fortune in Argentina. Under the name Bolo de Grangeneuve, he married Henriette Soumaille, a singer, who apparently was supporting him. He was arrested in Valparaiso, Chile, for stealing jewels and his wife arranged for his bail. After his release, he deserted her and returned to France.

In 1902, he was an agent for a champagne house in Lyons, and became friends to Madame Muller, the widow of a rich wine merchant. The wealth of Madame Muller loomed large in the mind eye of Paul Bolo, and he made every effort to gain her attention. In 1905, Bolo and the widow Muller were married and she moved from Bordeaux to Paris.

Bolo's good fortune came at a time when Parisian social life was recovering from the catastrophe of 1897. An organization of society ladies, the *Bazar de la Charite*, decided to hold their affair in the city rather than at one of the member's estate. A Madame Heine arranged for the group to use a site in the Rue Jean Gougon, near the Champs Elysees, and a number of wood and canvas stalls were built. This location was a small cul de sac and the only exit was in back of the stalls. One display was an early version of a movie picture projector. The lamp for the unit exploded and with 1,500 people in attendance, the stalls were destroyed. More than 120 people died in the flames. Most of the dead were women of the group.

* * * * * *

Now Paris was alive with a new group of social climbers, artists and rich young Americans seeking to marry titles to enhance their social position back home. This was the ideal time for Paul Bolo and his quest for recognition in the social and financial life of Paris. Prior to his good fortune, he was somewhat pompous and domineering, but now with his wife's fortune, he became unbearable. His early years had been spent organizing small businesses, and they all failed. He never had enough collateral for a bank loan, so now Bolo decided to ingratiate himself to those in the banking industry, thereby securing their help and consideration when it became necessary.

Bolo let it be known that he had money to invest and there were those who were willing and able to join in some of his ventures. Large sums of money were available for the right deal, and many deals were conceived and promoted.

The Bolos, with a home in Paris and one in Biarritz, entertained often and lavishly at both places. Many of their guests were well-connected in commerce and banking. Henri Bauer, director of the Perier Bank Paris, was included in their guest list.

After a trip to Cuba and the United States in February 1914, Bauer and Bolo met with executives of J.P. Morgan & Co. and were promised financial backing to start a bank in Cuba. The Morgan Bank had proposed providing some $25 million, however, after a closer look at the proposal, it withdrew its offer and the deal was finished.

There was another attempt to start a bank, this time the location would be in Spain. The Bank was to be a Catholic bank, as one of the partners was the Marquis Jules Della Chiesa, the younger brother of Pope Benedict. The Pope communicated his disapproval to the Papal Nuncio in Spain and that project also died.

* * * * * *

Paul Bolo was now in a poor financial position, and into this void came his introduction to the former Khedive of Egypt, Abbas Hilmi.

Abbas Hilmi Pacha hated the English and desired to chase them out of Egypt. The English had no position in Egypt until in 1875 they purchased the Egyptian stock of the Suez Canal. The remainder of the Canal stock was owned by the French government. Both the French and English were more than willing to bring in troops to protect their investment.

Egypt was by law an integral part of the Ottoman Empire, and Abbas Hilmi Pacha went to Constantinople (present day Istanbul, Turkey) for help to remove the English from Egypt. However, the war of 1914 forced the Turks to join the Central Powers and prevented them from coming to the aid of the ex-Khedive.

The English, in an attempt to legally justify their position in Egypt, made Prince Hussein Kamel Pacha the Sultan of Egypt. A Proclamation was issued December 18 to the effect that "Egypt is placed under the protection of His Majesty and will henceforth constitute a British protectorate. In view of the action of His Highness Abbas Hilmi Pacha, lately Khedive of Egypt, who has adhered to the King's enemies, His Majesty's government has seen fit to dispose him from the Khedivate. "

Egypt, after nearly four hundred years, ceased to be a part of the Ottoman Empire and the British government considered themselves trustees for the inhabitants of Egypt and pledged to defend the country against all aggressions.

In June 1914, Sadik Pacha, the personal aid to the Khedive, introduced Bolo to the Khedive in Paris. Bolo was quick to propose various schemes to support the Khedive in his efforts to dispel the British from Egypt. He offered to promote a plan whereby he could appeal to the French public to also support the Khedive against the British in the operation of the Suez Canal. The title of Pacha, given to civil or military officers of high rank by the Turks, was conferred to Bolo to enhance his position as being an advisor to the Khedive.

When the war began in August 1914, there was a pause in the activities of the ex-Khedive. The German army was meeting little resistance from the Belgian armed forces and the French armed forces. German forces were within 15 miles of Paris before they were halted and forced to withdraw. The standoff that followed created the need for other means and methods to overcome the opposition. For Germany, they decided to incite the French public to protest the war, after all, most of the fighting on the western front was on French soil.

Chapter 3

The Propagandists

Between December 1914 and October 1915, Bolo made three trips to Italy and six trips to Switzerland. Through his emissary Filippo Cavallini, who was in Milan, Italy, a telegram was sent to the ex-Khedive in Vienna, Austria requesting an urgent meeting in Rome. This was on Feb. 2, 1915. Sadik Pacha was also asked to be present.

The meeting took place in Rome where one Mahmud Pacha Yeghen, an Egyptian financier, was among those in attendance. Bolo convinced the ex-Khedive that he was ideal person to direct the program to bring France and Germany together. There was, of course, a need for preliminary operations to prepare for public opinion. The French press had to utilized, however, and that would require at a minimum $10 million, Bolo said.

Further meetings were held in Geneva and Zurich, Switzerland, with Sadik Pacha; the Austrian Theresa Hartmann for the ex-Khedive; Bolo's accountant, Darius Porchere in Paris; and Cavallini in Milan. Some of the information to Cavallini was addressed to "Mme. Cocchio," an alias he often used.

The most important of these meetings took place on March 16, 1915, at the Hotel Savoy in Zurich. Present at this meeting was the ex-Khedive, Mile Lusanges, Chefik Pacha and Fakir El Din. Those who came with Bolo were Cavallini, and Herr Erzberger, the German Central Party deputy, who was staying at the Hotel St. Gothard under the name of Adberger of Conogae.

The group could not agree on how to promote German propaganda to the French people. The following day, Sadik Pasha came and had a meeting with the ex-Khedive. They decided to try to purchase existing French newspapers, for they were numerous and many were run by Socialists who opposed the war.

Before separating, the two men arranged a special code for their scheme. The ex-Khedive would be known as "Marie," Sadik Pacha "the Doctor," and Bolo as "Richt." Money would be referred to as "samples." Cavallini would be the postal or middle man.

Sadik Pacha proceeded to Berlin and presented their plan to Von Jagow, the German Foreign Minister and Jagow agreed to pay $2.5 million in 10 monthly payments. Sadik returned to Vienna and telegraphed Cavallini to inform Bolo that they had been successful with Von

Jagow. Bolo did not like the idea of monthly payment amounts, however, the ex-Khedive directed him to proceed and gave Bolo full powers to buy newspapers in France.

On March 23, a special courier was sent from the Dresdner Bank in Berlin to Zurich to hand the first installment of the money to the ex-Khedive. Bolo was prevented from coming to Zurich and tried to get it through a friend. A telegram was sent to Cavallini in Milan – "Marie will only give samples to M. Richt himself."

If getting the money was going to be a problem, Bolo decided to give up the entire deal. Abbas Himli, the ex-Khedive, traveling with a passport in the name of Roustam, and Sadik met with Cavallini and presented three cheques: $150,000 on a Zurich bank and two others on banks in St. Gall and Fribourg. Abbas and Sadik met Bolo on April 13, 1915 in Zurich where Bolo complained about the amount of the checks.

It was arranged that funds would be sent to Paris from time to time, a method the ex-Khedive devised to protect his fortune. Sadik and Abbas were taking a commission of 10 percent on all funds they transferred in this manner. The total amount of money that went through the hands of these three persons is unknown, however, it was estimated to be close to $500,000.

By this time, Bolo was now a very important figure in the social and political affairs of Parisian society. The society paper *Tout Paris* wrote of Bolo: "Bolo Pacha, Chevalier of the Legion of Honour, Officer of the Academy, Officer of Agricultural Merit, Grand Cross and Foreign Order, Commander of Foreign Orders, Officer of three Foreign Orders, 17 Rue de Phalsbourg – telephone Wagram 8334 – second Wednesdays, and Villa Velleda, Biarritz; proprietor of the motor car and aeroplane."

The U.S. Undersecretary of State in Paris, Abel Ferry and his wife met the Bolos at a dinner party at the home of Deputie Meunier-Surcouf. Bolo's personal relationship with high government officials made him an important figure in Paris society.

The war was at a stalemate for most of 1915, however, the French Secret Service was alarmed at the amount of funds passing between persons in France and Switzerland. The funds for Bolo were delivered by courier and now he had to seek other means of transport. The neutrality of the United States and the tremendous amount of traffic in shipping and wireless communications among all of the combatants made the U.S. the ideal place to conceal many types of conspiracies.

* * * * * *

As the German industries expanded to other countries, they brought with them the base for a system of propaganda to enhance their influence with the local populations. They employed writers, speakers and newspapers which they subsidized to proclaim the superiority of German people and the German workers.

At the beginning of the war, there were 80,000 Germans living in Spain, unable to return to Germany. They were used to promote the cause of Germany against France and Britain.

There was also a revolution underway in Mexico, so the German propagandists were deeply involved in trying to create anti-American feeling along the border. Berlin supported 23 newspapers, supplied them with free paper at a cost of $50,000 a month.

Captain of the Uhlans Franz Von Papen was appointed both military attaché to Washington and Mexico City. This was in July 1914, before the war had begun. He went to Mexico City first before going on to Washington. In conversation with the German Minister, Rear Admiral Von Hintze, he proposed to organize German settlements and communities on a military plan for self defense.

He also voiced an opinion as to the attitude of loyalty for those of German origin, to whit, "Germans must remain Germans, to say they owe allegiance to the country of their adoption is sheer sentimentality. Any son of a German mother is a German forever."

The most fertile location for German propaganda was the United States. One organization, the National German-American Alliance, had a membership of more than 3 million. Few people realized at that time the extent of the progress of German-controlled industry in the United States. The Bosch Magneto Company and Telefunken controlled 50 percent of the country's battery ignition business. Also, 90 percent of the dyes used in this country were supplied by six German concerns. German money had built two high-powered radio transmitters, one at Sayville, Long Island, and the other at Tuckerton, N.J. German interests owned 30 percent of the sugar business of the Hawaiian Islands and through the Hamburg-American Ship Line, owned wharfs and docks in the port of St. Thomas, Virgin Islands.

The German ambassador Von Bernstorff had the funds to purchase whatever was needed to promote and aid the German war effort. It was estimated the ambassador had access to over $100 million in several New York City banks. In 1915 as the armies were digging in to consolidate their gains, various industries were gearing up to produce war supplies.

* * * * * *

In the United States, President Woodrow Wilson was campaigning for re-election and proclaimed the neutrality of the United States. The policies of the New York bankers, however, were destined to override the intentions of the President.

The actions of J.P. Morgan, Jr., were to emulate those of his grandfather, Junius Morgan. In 1870, when Paris was surrounded by German forces, J.S. Morgan & Co. agreed to float a $50 million loan for the French government. Two and a half decades later, with the German forces only 50 miles from Paris, J.P. Morgan & Co. under the leadership of J.P. Morgan, Jr., underwrote a $500 million loan to the French government. J.P. Morgan & Co. became the American agent of the Allied governments. The largest single listing with J.P. Morgan & Co. was the British 5-percent war loan of $10 billion. American bankers were also buying back American securities from abroad and selling foreign bonds to the American people.

Most of the foreign governments sent commissions to the United States to purchase supplies and soon most factories were in operation day and night to fulfill the orders. In 1915 and 1916, according to international law and the Hague Convention of 1907, a neutral nation could sell to any and all buyers. The Allies were spending some $10 million per day; the Central Powers spent very little on supplies for they had limited means of delivery.

The International Mercantile Marine Company was formed in 1902. J.P. Morgan, Sr., was the leader of the group which included both American and British capitalists. The combination included the following shipping lines: American Line, the Red Star, the White

Star, the Leyland, the Dominion and Inman lines. The White Star line and the Cunard were considered the pride of British shipping.

The object of Morgan, Sr., was to create an American marine fleet to compete with the fleets of other large industrial nations. In June 1914 the British Empire owned 47.7 percent of the entire world's sea-going steel tonnage, and American companies owned 4.3 percent. This new company gave American investors part ownership in over 50 percent of all world shipping and by agreement most of the ships could continue to fly the British flag. The future direction of American foreign policy was no longer in doubt.

The Morgan bank had just moved into its new building on the corner of Broad and Wall streets, when they were given the largest contract in the history of banking. The nations of Great Britain, France and Russia made the Morgan Bank their sole agent for the purchase of arms, ammunition and food supplies. The entire third floor of the building was the center of this operation.

There had always been groups that opposed the sale of arms to the warring nations in Europe. Some made peaceful public protest, while there were others who were violent in their actions. The German embassy in Washington, D.C., directed a group of agents located in New York City in many acts of sabotage against American plants that were producing steel and arms. The German military attaché in Washington, Captain Von Papen, was in charge of this operation. He had an official office at 11 Broadway in New York City, however, he ran his group of saboteurs from an old brownstone house at 123 West 15th Street. The building was managed by a former opera performer, Martha Held, who with two servants would cater to the visitors who appeared at all hours night and day. It was from here that they were given their assignments.

* * * * * *

J.P. Morgan, Jr., had become very visible in the public's perception of the arms trade, and some of his associates were concerned about his safety. On July 3, 1915 Morgan had house guests at his country estate on East Island near Glen Cove, Long Island. As the butler prepared to serve breakfast to the family and their weekend guests, he was confronted by an armed stranger in the hallway. In the struggle to disarm the gunman, Morgan was shot twice in the thigh and in the groin. The gunman was overpowered and captured.

In his confession, the gunman, Frank Holt, also admits to having set a bomb at the United States Senate on July 2, the day before he shot Morgan. Holt of Ithaca, N.Y., was a professor of French and German at Cornell University.

Soon after the shooting, Detective Frank McCahill and other detectives took the prisoner to the jail at Glen Cove, N.Y. During his interrogation, Holt said: "I decided to do two things. The first was to arouse public attention to the crime of selling munitions abroad, and to force Morgan, the most powerful man in this country, to withdraw his efforts and support in these matters."

This local matter now became a national event, and Holt was moved to the county jail in Mineola, N.Y. Dr. Guy Cleghorn of Mineola was summoned to the jail by Warden Hults to check on the physical condition of the prisoner, because he refused to eat or leave his bed. Hults feared that Holt may have taken poison.

Now that Holt was a prime suspect in other incidents of violence, police departments in New York City and Washington, D.C., were ready to find out if he had others assisting him, for there had been numerous incidents of arson and sabotage in American plants and on ships at sea. The interrogation was carried out for several hours, until Holt, exhausted, was unable to speak in a coherent manner.

On July 5, the second day after the attack on Morgan, Holt was confronted with the list of explosives he had purchased and also the locations he had used to make the bombs used in the Washington, D.C. explosion. Among the group of new interrogators was Chief William J. Flynn of the United State Secret Services.

Justice of the Peace William E. Luyster telephoned to Mineola to inform them of a mistake in the commitment papers. Holt was not held for the Grand Jury, but for a preliminary examination, therefore, his lawyer could and did refuse to permit any more questions from the police. On July 6, as the evidence against Holt continued to increase, he became morose and showed signs of depression. Dr. Cleghorn and Warden Hults could not persuade the prisoner to take food, and they had his belt and suspenders removed from the cell.

Deputy Jerry Ryan was assigned the task of watching the prisoner for the night. The cell door was left unlocked to assure fast entry in an emergency. About 10:30 p.m., Deputy Ryan heard a noise in the cell block. Thinking that Holt was asleep, Ryan went to investigate. On his way back to Holt's cell, he heard a loud sound like a gun shot. The cell was vacant and there was no sign of the prisoner. The cell was on an upper tier. Deputy Ryan rushed down the stairs to go sound an alarm when he stumbled on the body of Holt.

Warden Hults and Dr. Cleghorn were summoned to the jail. About 1 a.m. that night, Dr. Cleghorn had the body moved to Cornell's morgue in Hempstead, Long Island, and performed an autopsy. The autopsy report gave the cause of death as massive skull fracture. Holt must have landed on the cement floor head first from a fall of almost 20 feet. Ten days after the incident, an inquest was held by the Nassau County coroner and the death was ruled a suicide.

* * * * * *

There were others who also protested against the policy of American industry supplying war materials to Britain, Russia and France. William Jennings Bryant resigned his position as Secretary of State in order to join the National Peace Council, a group that was organized to prevent the shipment of war supplies to Europe. In a public letter to President Wilson, they cited Article V of the 1907 Hague Convention, which states, "Belligerents are forbidden to use neutral ports and waters as a base of operations against their adversaries." They listed the names of nine ships and the ports where they were being loaded with contraband supplies. Their letter also accused the British and French governments of using the docks of the White Star and Fabre lines to store and load war supplies on their ships.

The International Mercantile Marine Company was chartered in the state of New Jersey, however, all of the vessels owned by the Morgan Group were, by agreement, considered as part of the British Mercantile Marine. The terms of the agreement were disclosed in a speech in Sheffield by Gerald <u>Balfour</u>, president of the British Board of Trade. He said: "The Cunard line pledged themselves to remain in every respect a British company managed by British directors – the shares not to be transferred to any but British subjects. Their ships were to be officered by British officers." The line also engaged to construct two vessels of 24 to 25 knots, which, as well as the entire Cunard fleet, the admiralty would have the right to charter or purchase at any time on terms fixed in the agreement. The money for the construction of the fast steamers would be advanced to the company at the rate of 2 ¾ percent interest, while in lieu of the present admiralty subvention -- 28,000 pounds a year for the contingent use of three ships – the company would receive 150,000 pounds a year. With Pierpont Morgan, the head of the shipping combination, who had shown the utmost readiness to meet the wishes of his majesty's government, it had been agreed that the British companies in the combination should remain British, not merely in name, but in reality. The majority of their directors were to be British subjects.

All their ships now flying the British flag were to continue to fly it, and at least one-half of those hereafter to be built for the combination would likewise fly British colors, be commanded by British officers and manned in reasonable proportion by British sailors. On the other hand, the combined companies would continue to be treated, as heretofore, on a footing of equality with other British companies in respect of any services, whether postal, military, or naval, which his majesty's government might require from the British Mercantile Marine. It had been further stipulated that in the event of the combination pursuing a policy hostile to our mercantile marine or to British trade, the King's government should have the right to terminate the agreement.

The National Peace Council's request for a public inquiry on the Unneutral Acts in Progress went unheeded.

Chapter 4

Bolo Comes to America

On February 21, 1916 at 1:15 a.m. the German army began its assault on the forts at Verdun. On February 22 at 10:30 a.m. the S.S. Lafayette from France was nudged into the quay in the port of New York. Among the passengers coming ashore were Charles Bertelli, French correspondent for the Hearst papers; Mme. Marian Buzenete, shop owner at 714 Fifth Avenue – and Paul Marie Bolo Pacha.

After clearing customs, Bolo went by taxi to the Plaza Hotel in midtown Manhattan. From shipboard, Bolo had cabled Adolph Pavenstedt, a partner in G. Amsinck & Co., to contact him as soon as possible at the Plaza Hotel. Bolo and Pavenstedt knew each other, having met while both were in Cuba in 1914. Pavenstedt arrived at the Plaza around 6 p.m. and after a few pleasantries, Bolo stated he needed some help with a business matter of great importance.

"I have a contract to purchase the controlling stock of *La Journal,* one of the largest newspapers in Paris, from Senator Humbert, Senator Charles and I need quite a large sum of money. I hope as a friend you will help me," Bolo said. He gave Pavenstedt a piece of paper which he said was the contract, and he wanted him to study it. That was the extent of their evening visit. The contract was returned the following day, and the terms were discussed between the two. Bolo was seeking 10 million francs ($1.7 million) to buy *La Journal* and three other newspapers, to which Pavenstedt replied, "I am a business man and what you are asking me is out of the question. I don't know any financiers or bankers that would show interest in a proposition such as this."

With the help of Senator Humbert, Bolo stated, "Our mission is to bring public opinion in France – through the press – to pressure for early peace. France is bleeding to death." Pavenstedt replied, "You may get a man like Henry Ford, who has sentimental peace ideas in his business, but not this as a business proposition."

After lunch at the Downtown Club, the two men had the following conversation:

Bolo: "I can't get on here. I don't know the people, I don't know the language. You must help me get this money."

21

Pavenstedt: "I don't know who to approach with this thing. I can't go to Wall Street with a proposal like this. It is absolutely unbusiness-like."

Bolo: "Don't you know somebody? Can't you think of somebody who would be interested in this thing?"

Pavenstedt: "I will candidly tell you, I only know one man who I think would be interested in this, and that is Count Bernstorff, the German ambassador. Would you have any objections to me speaking to him about this?"

Bolo: "I don't know any of these people here. I leave that to you. I only deal with you. You do whatever you think, where you can get the money."

Later that afternoon, Count Bernstorff was informed that a member of the French government had an emissary here in New York and he was given certain facts of Bolo's story. The ambassador instructed Pavenstedt to come to the Washington embassy the following day. Bernstorff knew of Senator Humbert by name, and he also was aware that *Le Journal* was a large paper in Paris. "It would be a great thing for me if we could do something to change the tone of the people of France toward a peaceful solution to end the war."

He thought the sum was large, but he was interested. "I will have to think it over, and I will be in New York in a few days and I will let you know. Come around and see me at the Ritz Hotel when I get there." This meeting with the ambassador occurred on the 24th of February.

While Pavenstedt was in Washington, Bolo visited the New York Branch office of the Royal Bank of Canada. Henri Bauer of Perier & Co. of Paris had sent a letter of introduction for Bolo to R.E. Jones at the Royal Bank of Canada, and a letter of credit for Bolo to Pavenstedt's company. The visit to the Royal Bank of Canada was to open an account in his name and to explore the possibility of purchasing large quantities of paper for the *Le Journal* and other French papers.

Jones, the New York agent, wired C.E. Neill at the Montreal office with the information, asking if a contract was possible. Neill passed the telegram on to F.F. Walker, managing director of the bank, for his opinion on such a large order of 20,000 tons. Walker replied that the order could be filled, however, payments must be made at a Canadian or American port; delivery to a European port was out of the question.

Charles Bertelli, the French correspondent for Hearst newspapers, arrived on the same steamer as Bolo and introduced him to William Randolph Hearst, who later invited Bolo and Bertelli to have lunch with him and discuss the conditions in France. Bertelli arrived in New York on the S.S. Lafayette with Bolo and sought some exchange between Hearst papers and various French publishers. Hearst was not too impressed by Bolo. He did show an interest in the paper purchase, however, for he was having a problem with his supplies at the time. Hearst's mother stopped giving him financial assistance at this time, and his suppliers were about to sue him. He could only obtain paper by sending a check with his order.

Bertelli made numerous attempts to get laudatory items on Hearst in several French papers, however, the French postal censor blocked all efforts for Hearst was considered by them to be pro-German. Later on there were articles in both *Le Journal* and *La Victoire* proclaiming the support of Hearst for the people of France.

On Feb. 27, Pavenstedt returned to New York from Washington, D.C., and told Bolo of his interview with Count Bernstorff. On Feb. 29, Herr Von Jagow, the German Foreign Minister, cabled Bernstorff: "Agree to loan, but only if peace action seems to you a really serious project, as the provision of money in New York is for us at present extraordinarily difficult. If Russia or Italy is meant, nothing is to be done as amount is too small to affect Russia and Italy would not justify so large an expenditure."

On March 2 at the Ritz-Carlton in New York, Count Bernstorff and Pavenstedt met, at which time they decided on how to complete the transfer of the funds. Hugo Schmidt, agent for Deutsche Bank, New York, would supply the funds to Pavenstedt. Schmidt and Pavenstedt would arrange the details together. The funds would be sent to G. Amsinck & Co., informed his cashier : "If you get a check for $250,000 here from Guaranty Trust Company, put it in our deposit to the order of G. Amsinck & Co., then you write off the same amount, a check to the Royal Bank of Canada, our own check, on our own bank, Bank of New York, with a letter saying we pay you this money for the account of Mr. Bolo Pacha, placed to his credit." Bolo had also sent a letter to G. Amsinck & Co: "You will receive for my account sums of money which A. Pavenstedt knows the amount. Will you be good enough to apply them to the credit of my account at the New York Branch of the Royal Bank of Canada."

Hugo Schmidt began to dispense the funds as they were released to him from the Deutsche Bank of Berlin.

March 13 -- $500,000 from Guarantee Trust Co. to G. Amsinck & Co.
March 17 -- $300,000 from Guarantee Trust co. to G. Amsinck & Co.
March 21 -- $300,000 from National Park Bank to G. Amsinck & Co.
March 25 -- $200,000 from Guarantee Trust Co. to G. Amsinck & Co.
April 1   -- $283,500 from National Park Bank to G. Amsinck & Co.
April 1   -- $200,000 from Guarantee Trust Co. to G. Amsinck & Co.

As these checks arrived, G. Amsinck & Co. sent checks for equal amounts to the Royal Bank of Canada for credit to the account of Paul Bolo-Pacha.

The day after the first check arrived, Bolo sent the bank the following letter of instructions.

New York, March 14, 1916
The Royal Bank of Canada, New York

Gentlemen:

You will receive from Messrs. G. Amsinck & Co. deposits for the credit of my account with you, which deposits will reach an aggregate amount of about $1,700,000, which I wish you to utilize in the following manner.

First, immediately on receipt of the first amount on account of this sum pay to Messrs. J.P. Morgan & Co., New York City, the sum of $170,090.60, to be placed to the credit of the account with those of Senator Charles Humbert, Paris.

Second, establish on your books a credit of $5,000.00 good until May 31, in favor of Mr. Jules Bois, Biltmore Hotel, this amount to be utilized by him to debit of my account, according to his needs and the unused balance to be returned to me.

Shelby F. Westbrook

Third, transfer to the credit of my wife, Mme. Bolo with agency M of the Comptoir National D'Escompte De Paris a sum of about $534,000, to be debited to account as such transfers are made by you at best rate and by small accounts.

Fourth, you will hold, subject to my instructions only when all payments are complete, a balance of not less than $1,000,000.

Yours Truly,
Bolo Pacha

Marian Buzenet owned a boutique at 714 Fifth Avenue and was also a passenger on the ship with Bolo and Bertelli. One of her models, Sonia Ouff, made a trip to France at Bolo's request and also at his expense.

William Randolph Hearst gave a dinner party at his home on Riverside Drive and invited several notable persons to meet Bolo. Judge Elbert H. Gary, chairman of the board of U.S. Steel was one of the guests. C.V. Van Anda, managing editor of *The New York Times*, was also in attendance. After the dinner party, 12 in all went to the theatre.

Prior to Bolo's departure from New York for France, Bertelli arranged a dinner party at Sherry's, the choice of the rich and famous for social events. The lavish affair was attended by 125 guests. Some of those included Mr. and Mrs. Hearst, Bertelli, Jules Bois, A. Pavenstedt and C.V. Van Anda.

Jules Bois, author and lecturer, was in the United States at the request of the French officials to promote American aid for France. The party was very expensive and Bolo picked up the check. He wanted to show his American guests that this was the kind of party he gave for his friends in Paris. On the 17th of March, after 23 days in New York, Bolo departed for France.

The final transfer of funds from G. Amsinck & Co. to the Royal Bank of Canada was on April 3, 1916. There was a balance of $1 million in the account. Bolo contacted Morgan, Harjes & Co. in Paris and had $1 million from the Royal Bank of Canada placed in a special deposit account at J.P. Morgan & Co., New York, at 2 ½ percent interest. The deposit to be payable six months from the day of receipt: October 14, 1916.

* * * * * *

The fighting at Verdun was intense, and public attention was riveted on the possible outcome. The comings and goings of people like Bolo Pacha was of no interest. The siege of Verdun by the German army would last for over five months. The British Army in their effort to ease the pressure on the French Army, began their attack on the German positions at the Somme River. The battles of Verdun and the Somme were the most important events of the year 1916.

The terror on the front lines and the arduous living conditions of the troops added a new dimension of the conflict for the general public. Over 2 million men were either killed, wounded or missing in the Verdun and Somme engagements. In France, hospitals were so overcrowded that the government had to use the upper stories of the larger schools to house the wounded.

The winter of 1916-17 was a test of spirit for the general public, and this test applied to the people of Germany as well as the people of Britain and France. The men needed to till the fields for food supplies. Those needed to mine the coal for heat and fuel for utilities and light were away in the army. In Germany, it was known as the "cabbage winter," cabbage being the main source of food. There was also a shortage of coal for heat. In France, there was hardly a home without the loss of a family member. A soldier on leave often returned to find his home unheated, no lights and food rationed. The scarcity of coal and medical supplies, as well as the shortage of food, intensified the spread of the Spanish flu epidemic.

The French High Command appointed General Robert N. Nivelle as the Commander-in-Chief of the French armies, and the result was a near disaster for the French army. After three winters in the trenches, the men in the army were tired, lonely for their families and, after hearing rumors of peace talks, were reluctant to go on any but defensive maneuvers.

America declared war against Germany on April 6, 1917.

On May 3, the French 21st Division of Colonial Infantry refused to obey their officers. Those men selected as spokespersons for the men were arrested and charged with mutiny. The military command refused to negotiate with the written demands of the men and other regiments joined the protest.

The French Secret Service reports to army headquarters were fraught with incidences of units refusing to obey orders. More than 20,000 Frenchmen deserted outright and a total of 54 divisions were involved. It was clear that General Nivelle had lost the support of the army and he was replaced by General Petain. Command in the army was restored, but at a terrible price. Twenty-three mutineers were officially shot and another 250 were sent into a quiet sector and slaughtered by their own artillery.

The German high command had decided to alter their plans at the time that the French army was having their problems. Operation "Alberich" would withdraw the army to better defense positions on the western front called the Hindenburg Line. This would shorten the area defended and free 20 divisions for reserves. There were reports suggesting that the unrest in the French and Russian armies was due to German propaganda, which they disseminated so they had time to rest their own soldiers.

The propaganda campaign against Russia was promoted through Geneva, Switzerland; Copenhagen, Denmark; and Stockholm, Sweden. One item of instruction was as follows:

Order of March 2, 1917

The Imperial Bank to all Representatives of German Banks in Switzerland.

By the present we inform you that demands for money for pacifist propaganda in Russia are about to be made from that country via Finland. These demands will be made by the following persons: Lenin, Zinovieff, Kameneff, Trotsky, Sumenson, Koslovsky, Kolontai, Sivers, and Mercain, whose accounts have been opened by our order No. 2754 in the agencies of the private German banking establishments in Sweden, Norway and Switzerland.

All these demands must be confirmed by one of two signatures: Dirschau or Wolkenburg. At sight of these authorized signatures, the demands of the above-mentioned propagandists in Russia will be considered as regular and immediately executed.

No. 7433 Imperial Bank

Chapter 5

Le Bonnet Rouge

Illiteracy was rampant throughout Russia and the propaganda campaign there was carried out by skilled political agitators.

In France, however, the newspapers were the primary source of information to the public and several were used to help promote unrest in the French army. The French Secret Service had begun to trace the flow of large sums of funds from Switzerland to several individuals and their papers. The *Tranchee Republicaine*, *Les Nations*, *Le Journal*, and the *Bonnet Rouge* were the most active in promoting German propaganda. The *Bonnet Rouge* was not one of the large Parisian papers, however, it was found in every kiosk on the more popular streets in Paris. The publisher, Vigo Almereyda, had a history of anti-government activities.

Almeyreda was sentenced to two months imprisonment in 1900 for theft; to a year's imprisonment in 1901 for the manufacture of explosives; to three years for incitement to murder, and in 1908 and again in 1910 he was arrested and convicted of attempted sabotage against the military.

The Radical Socialist Party under the leadership of Caillaux and Jean-Louis Malvy, Minister of the Interior, was opposing the law requiring all young men to serve three years in the military, as well as the repeal of the income tax law. The trial of Madame Caillaux for the murder of Gaston Calmette was the event that brought these two men together. At the beginning of the trial, the *Bonnet Rouge* was a weekly publication, and was highly supportive of Madame Caillaux.

Joseph Caillaux was himself under criticism for some of his policies that concerned the settlement with Germany in 1911 at Agadir, Morocco. In order to maintain some public support for his wife, he donated $7,000 to *Le Bonnet Rouge* which enabled the paper to be published daily.

Even though Madame Caillaux was acquitted, Caillaux resigned his Senate seat after the trial, which left Malvy as the leader of the Radical Socialist Party. The publication of the paper was suspended by the military authorities for seditious articles. The censors had banned over 1,400 columns between 1915 and 1917, yet permitted the paper to continue to publish. Almereyda had written articles that were both anti-British and unpatriotic. However, he was a frequent visitor to the office of Malvy, and seemed above the law. The military took command when a secret document concerning French forces in Saloniki was found in the safe of *Le Bonnet Rouge*. Almereyda was arrested on charges of sedition and placed in jail. However, he was not under military guard in jail – he was under the civil authorities, in this case, his friend Malvy's Interior Department.

Vigo Almereyda was never brought to trial. He was found dead in his prison cell. The facts surrounding this event were never fully explained. One report said he hanged himself with his own shoe laces, while another said he died from an overdose of morphine.

* * * * * *

In September 1914, the German Army had swept across Belgium and toward Paris. To defend Paris, the French planned a line of defense at the Marne River. General Clergerie devised a means to transport reserve troops to the front. He organized 600 Paris Taxi Cabs to move 6,000 men to the Marne. Each cab would carry five men and make two trips. This was a successful operation, and not only saved Paris, it changed the entire course of World War I.

In 1916, General Clergerie was the Military Governor of Paris. His bureau of counter-espionage under the command of Major Baudier, had Caillaux and some of his associates under surveillance.

As the Interior Minister, Malvy was incensed by the action of the Military Bureau. Major Baudier was summoned to meet at Malvy's office, at which time he was told: "I have demanded that you shall leave the Military Government of Paris because the action of your Bureau is not in accord with the attitude which I wish to give to the Police of the Minister of the Interior. The line adopted by the Military Government of Paris is opposed to my view. I have decided to change the whole personnel of the Military Government, the Governor, his Chief of Staff, and yourself."

This attitude of the Ministry of the Interior allowed the Propagandist to inspire mutinies in the army and unrest in certain areas in the rear. The Police services were poor in containing the actions of those individuals who were listed in their archives as being dangerous to National Defense. This book was known as Carnet-B, the Red Book. It was produced in six copies and one copy went to Malvy, who failed to put an end to treasonable propaganda.

The Military Governor of Paris, General Auguste Dubail, assigned Captain Pierre Bouchardon and Lieutenant Andre Mornet to investigate why some of the persons listed in Carnet-B were given passports to travel frequently to Switzerland. It was known that large sums of German Funds were coming from Switzerland to finance defeatist propaganda in France.

Captain Bouchardon and Lieutenant Mornet were the Prosecution Team that convicted Margaretha Zelle, better known as Mata Hari, of being a spy, which resulted in her being executed by a firing squad. Their new investigations began with cabinet members of the Ministry of the Interior.

Maunoury, the former Director of the Cabinet of the prefect of Police, was asked about his knowledge of funds coming from Switzerland and any complicity on his part. He often boasted that he was the real Prefect of Police.

Jean Leymarie, the Chief of Staff in the Ministry of the Interior, was charged with Breaches of the Trading with the Enemy Acts. No charges are made with the Transfer of the Prefect of Police and the Surete General.

George Clemenceau, now the Prime Minister, was determined to eradicate all signs of corruption within the Government. As a former reporter and now part owner of a newspaper, *L Homme Enchaine*, he was irate that French newspapers were being used to promote defeatism among the public, financed with German funds.

The first paper to feel the wrath of the Military was *Le Bonnet Rouge*. The Director plus all of the Reporters and Staff were under detention. Duval, the Director, made more than twenty visits to Switzerland to receive checks from a German Banker named Marx from Mannheim. The checks totaled close to $200,000. The paper was also receiving funds from the Ministry of the Interior.

* * * * * *

With the members of *Le Bonnet Rouge* under detention, the Military Secret Service now focused their attention on the newspaper *Le Journal*.

The French Secret Service agent in Switzerland, M. Casella, who was also the correspondent for the Paris paper *Matin*, was asked to comment on what was called the "Affaire of the Pachas." Near the close of 1916, the Swiss Police seized documents that showed large sums of money were given in Switzerland to German Agents.

Arrested was Malomed Yaghen Pacha who was the Minister of the Khedivial Civil List. The Civil List determined who received funds and at what amounts. Paul Bolo made definite business arrangements with the Pachas in either September or October 1914. The Casella report that detailed the activities of Bolo and the Pachas was filed in April 1917. The report did not reach the examining magistrate, Captain Bouchardon until October 1917.

The Military Police went to the Grand Hotel where Bolo was staying, and after two hours of interrogation, he was placed under arrest. The prisoner, because of his illness, appealed to the Police for a respite of two days before being taken to prison. This was refused.

A private ambulance was called, and Bolo was wrapped in blankets, placed on a stretcher and taken to Fresne jail where he was placed in a hospital cell.

Chapter 6

Bolo On Trial

After Bolo Pacha was arraigned on charges of treason, it was the job of the prosecutors to present to the court the evidence to prove their case. The French Secret Service knew that large sums of funds were coming from Switzerland, for they had intercepted some of these funds. However, when the Swiss were asked for information on these items they refused to cooperate. Their response was "These are political matters," and by the banking laws of their country, they could not release any information.

When questioned about the large sums of funds he had received from the United States, Bolo declared he had invested in American industries and they were making millions producing war materials for the allies. When he was asked to name the companies he had invested in, he could not name a single one.

The Military government of Paris had documents showing that J.P. Morgan of New York had transferred more than $2 million to Bolo through their Paris branch, Morgan Harjes & Company. They had no knowledge of the actual sources of the funds. The French Ambassador to the United States, M.J.J. Jusserand, made an appeal to the Attorney General of New York for aid in finding the real source of these funds.

With the approval of the special assistant to the U.S. Attorney General, Alfred Becker, Deputy Attorney General of New York was placed in charge of the investigation. Perley Morse & Company, certified public accountants, was selected to audit all the accounts relating to Bolo's finances in the U.S.

The French government wanted a log of all the messages and the names of the operators that were involved. The messages referred to were sent before the U.S. entered the conflict. The wireless stations used for trans-Atlantic communications were German-built, but were taken over by the U.S. government at the beginning of the war and put under control of the Navy. Collecting the navy records was rather time-consuming, for some of the Navy operators had been transferred to other stations.

The Perley Morse Company received their instructions on September 12, 1917 and within nine days, reported a complete record of Bolo's transactions through 10 different banks in the U.S., Canada and France prior to the United States' entry into the war.

Armed with two names – Adolph Pavenstedt and Hugo Schmidt – Attorney General Becker had to determine if the two individuals were still in New York City. Both had lived at a German club before the U.S. declared war on Germany. Afterward, Schmidt moved to 112 Central Park South and Pavenstedt moved to the Plaza Hotel. Though German nationals, the men moved freely around the city.

Subpoenas were issued to Pavenstedt and Schmidt at the beginning of October in 1917 for depositions on the financial affairs of Bolo Pacha.

With the arrest of Bolo for possible treason, police teams were sent to his homes at Villa Velleda, Biarritz; 17 Rue De Phalsbourg, Paris; and his suite at the Grand Hotel Paris. They gathered items including check studs, documents and correspondence. The charges filed were covered by nine different clauses of the Military and Criminal Code. His co-ownership with Senator Charles Humbert of *Le Journal* was also under investigation. The paper had been purchased by P. Lenoir and his partner Desouches, and then a half share was sold to Senator Humbert. There was evidence that the funds used by Lenoir and Desouches were of German origin and were from a source in Switzerland.

The most compelling event of all was the indictment of the former Prime Minister Joseph Caillaux for crimes against the security of the state, falling under article 12 of the constitution of 1875. The charges were based on a dossier of over 7,000 documents. On December 24, 1917, a resolution was passed by the French Chamber of Deputies, suspending the Parliamentary Immunity of Caillaux by a vote of 396 to two. The decision of the French Government to bring Caillaux before a court-martial for "endangering the security of the state" was the most important non-military event in France since the war began.

* * * * * *

On February 4, 1918, Bolo Pacha's trial began in the Seine Assize Court. A group of soldiers with fixed bayonets were stationed at the raised dais awaiting the entrance of the seven officers who form the Military Board of the Court. The Presiding Officer is Colonel Voyer, and as he and the others line up behind their seats, Bolo Pacha and his accountant Porchere are led into the dock by Military Escort.

The indictments were three – against Bolo for intelligence with the enemy; against Porchere for commerce with the enemy, and against Cavallini for complicity. Cavallini was being tried in absentia, as he was under arrest in Italy outside French Jurisdiction.

After the indictments had been read, the roll-call of witnesses began. Many of the witnesses called for the defense failed to answer to their names. Caillaux was called as a defense witness in Bolo's trial as he himself was in jail awaiting trial on similar charges. Other witnesses were in Switzerland and in the United States. The defense asked for dismissal of all charges or a delay of trial until they could establish a connection with the trial of Caillaux. The Court refused to grant an adjournment and the Military Prosecutor presented their case against the Defendants.

The charges were that Bolo had made an effort to buy a controlling interest in several French newspapers, namely the *Journal*, the *Rappel*, the *Figaro* and the most important newspaper in France, the *Temps*. The funds to accomplish these purchases came from two locations but had the same source, the Deutsche Bank. They were traced from Switzerland, to the ex-Khedive, to

Cavallini, and then to Bolo. The ex-Khedive and Cavallini both received a fee of 10 percent of the funds they handled.

From America, Hugo Schmidt the New York agent of the Deutsche Bank, named some of the banks that held large accounts of the German Funds before America entered the war. The funds were administered by Schmidt, but they were controlled by the German Ambassador Count Von Bernstorff from Washington D.C.

Colonel Voyer formally charged the prisoners and called upon Bolo to say what he wanted to say in his defense. Speaking in a low tone while fingering his eyeglasses, Bolo said, "I am not a traitor. I am quite willing to die, but I am not a traitor."

The Defense Counsel for Bolo, Albert Sallie, said none of the evidence against Bolo was worthy of attention. He raised the point that the article of the Penal Code under which Bolo was charged referred exclusively to acts committed in the field. He went farther and claimed that the prosecution had to establish that both in intention and in fact Bolo had been a traitor. The rights of the defendants were violated, he said, by the Military Governor of Paris, General Dubail, by writing of the "Treason of Bolo and Cavallini" before the report of the Examining Magistrate had been made.

The trial of Bolo Pacha produced a list of witnesses who were prominent in government positions, but none more so than Joseph Caillaux. The day he was called to testify there was not a spare seat in the courtroom. Caillaux said he first met Bolo in 1911, when he was Prime Minister. However, he denied knowledge of Bolo's travels to the U.S., although he admitted he maintained business relations with him until his arrest.

Defense counsel Sallie asked the Court, "Why is Caillaux not here in the Dock with Bolo? I know if he were here Bolo would be acquitted. It is because of a desire to shield the man who was powerful yesterday and who maybe powerful tomorrow, because the politicians desire to reserve for him a more comfortable fate before another Court."

The case against the defendants remained in limbo for several months because the Swiss government considered the matter to be political and therefore would not release any information to the French Government.

In December 1917, the French ambassador made a request to the New York State Attorney General for any records from American banks that had any connections with Bolo. Alfred Becker, Deputy Attorney General, hired the Perley Morse Company of New York to handle the investigation.

Within one month the French Ambassador, J.J. Jusserand, had transcripts and photographs with the records of transactions by German banks in New York. These records showed that Bolo received more than $2 million from the banks in America. The primary source of these funds was traced back to Hugo Schmidt and the Deutsche Bank of Germany.

The prosecution presented its collection of cablegrams, payments into banks by Germany, and payments to Bolo's credit of the same amounts in his own accounts. And all of the events occurred at the time Bolo was visiting in the United States. Those who were sitting in court felt they were watching a dead man. Defense Consul Sallie was unable to explain or dispute those documents.

Colonel Voyer, the presiding judge, putting on his kepi (a cap with a flat circular top and visor, worn by the French army), announced that the proceeding of the military court was over. French Military Law requires that once the evidence and closing speeches have been given, the court shall retire to consider its verdict. The seven officers, varying from Colonel to Sergeant, filed out of court to the judge's room.

The Judges were absent from the court for almost 45 minutes. With the sound of *Le Conseil*, every one rose as the judges returned and entered the court. On reaching their seats, they remained standing. Colonel Voyer removed his kepi and the other judges followed suit. He read the 11 questions which required affirmative or negative answers. "Is the accused Bolo guilty of charge number one, etc.?" and 11 times, the answer was guilty.

Having announced the judges' decision, Colonel Voyer put on his kepi, as did the other members of the court. With absolute silence in the room, he began, "in the name of the French people Bolo was found guilty of treason against France by reason of his dealing with the enemy and they sentenced him to death." Bolo received the news of his sentence with outward calm and felt he had grounds for an appeal.

Monsignor Bolo, the brother of the prisoner, had also appealed to President Poincare to save his brother's life. There was no response from the president's office. The Monsignor then visited the prison and left with the warden a new suit of clothes and a pair of white gloves for his brother.

At 5 a.m. on April 17 at the Sante Prison, General DuBail, Governor of Paris, Capt. Bouchardon and Dr. Socquet proceeded to Bolo's cell. Bolo dressed himself with great care in the black suit. A barber was called in to shave him and curl his moustache. He also took two white handkerchiefs and placed them on his heart as final souvenirs from his wife and his brother.

The prisoner received communion from the chaplain, then was escorted to a car where he was driven to Vincennes.

The firing squad was already in place and waiting for the victim. The squad was composed of 12 soldiers, commanded by a Lieutenant. The prisoner was bound to the stake, his eyes were bandaged and the execution was carried out.

Chapter 7

Joseph Caillaux On Trial

The trial of Bolo was just the first of several to follow. The attempt by Germany to destroy the will of the French to continue the war was part of a large system of propaganda.

The person who had been a witness for the defense in the "Affaire of the Pachas" where treason was the charge, had yet to face the court in his own defense. The presence of this person, Joseph Caillaux, overshadowed the men on trial. To some, he had the power of a Richelieu, and to others, the aura of a Svengali.

The travels of Caillaux had taken him to Italy, Argentina, and Switzerland. He was born in Le Mans, March 30, 1863, to a wealthy family. His father was an engineer and also a deputy in a provincial government. His father served as Minister of Public words and later as Minister of Finance from 1874 to 1877. Caillaux was educated in law and economics and in 1886 he was employed in the Ministry of Finance. In 1898 he ran for Political office and was elected to the Chamber of Deputies. He was appointed to the post once held by his father, Minister of Finance.

In 1911, a dispute occurred between France and Germany over their control in the African colonies. The French had marched on Fez Morocco, and Germany demanded a settlement on their interest in the area. The German cruiser Panther was sent to the port of Agadir Morocco to challenge the French, and it created an international crisis.

Caillaux had just become Prime Minister, and so it was up to his office along with the Foreign Minister to try and reach an agreement with the German government.

Soon after a settlement was reached with Germany, rumors began to surface that French interests were not being protected to the fullest. There were hints that Caillaux had used his position to make investments on the French Stock Exchange through certain bankers. He held positions at various banks and he was using his political power to enhance his wealth. When it became apparent that he had made concessions to the Germans that the Foreign Minister was unaware of, his tenure as Prime Minister came to its end.

Having served as Minister of Finance under three different presidents, Caillaux was well known to the international bankers of Europe. However, his arrogance alienated most of his colleagues because he ignored their advice on many policy decisions.

* * * * * *

However, ultimately it was personal problems – not the political ones – that made a profound impact on the life of Caillaux. His second marriage was the result of an adulterous liaison. As revealed during Mme. Caillaux's trial, there were a series of letters between Caillaux and Henriette, his second wife, which they exchanged before his divorce from his first wife.

Caillaux wed Henriette in 1911 just before he became Prime Minister, and during the crisis in Morocco, there were a series of letters that were coded messages to Henriette. In January 1914 – in the run-up to Henriette's shooting Calmette – the *Figaro* began to run a series of articles on the Minister of Finance and his relationship with banks that made profits on decisions made by his department while he still held positions and retained his salary as president and administrator of Credit Focier Argentin and Credit Foncier Egyptian.

These attacks against Caillaux were presented several times weekly. Georges Clemenceau, the Prime Minister, was hesitant to bring charges against his former colleague and at one point requested he leave the country. Caillaux declined to take this advice and the Governor General of Paris, General Dubail, made the demand for the suspension of Caillaux's Parliamentary Immunity.

Endangering the security of the State were the charges that Caillaux had to defend himself against before the members of the Chamber of Deputies. The text of the Governor General's address to Parliament began thus: "In the course of the examination of the cases of intelligence and commerce with the enemy, at present under the consideration of the Military and Civil Legal Authorities, there has been discovered at the homes of nearly all the accused persons a great number of letters from Caillaux, which leave no doubt as to the nature of the relations between him and those accused."

He then began to list the many letters between Caillaux and Bolo Pacha, and cited the friendly relations between Almereyda, his staff at *Le Bonnet Rouge* and the former Prime Minister, as well as several trips to Italy where he met with the German agent Cavallini.

The demand to prosecute Caillaux on a charge of treason was presented to a committee of the chamber of deputies on December 13, 1917. On the recommendation of the committee, the Chamber of Deputies with a vote of 396 to 2 endorsed the suspension of Parliamentary Immunity of Caillaux. This decision was made on December 24, 1917.

There were no vacant seats in the house when Caillaux with an impassioned two-hour speech presented his defense to the accusations brought against him.

"Parliamentary procedure at last enables me to utter here at this tribune a deep cry of indignation. If I am forced to make political allusions, I will only do so in the measure required by my defense. People have spoken of sinister combinations, of mysterious intrigues, which had as aim to change the political orientation of France and to detach her from her Allies. Well, with all my soul, all my strength, and all my being. I protest. Never have I sought to draw night to the enemy, and if attempts have been made to get me to do so, I have spurned them away with my Boot immediately I saw them. I have never indulged in any ambiguous intrigue nor taken any underground paths."

"It is good to suffer for one's ideas when one's act is glorious, when one has the certainty of duty done, and when one is sure of having had in view nothing but the Greatness and Triumph of France."

On January 16, 1918, Colonel Chiapirone arrived in Paris with the documents and securities seized in Caillaux's safe deposit box at the Banea Di Sconto in Florence, Italy. The documents were taken to the room of Captain Bouchardon, the examining Magistrate, at the Palais De Justice.

Colonel Chiapirone, Chief of the Rome Military Tribunal, released all of the contents of the safe and he also gave evidence of the actions of Caillaux and the doings by Cavallini in Paris as well as in Rome. The Rome Military Tribunal had jurisdiction over the whole of Italy. Chiapirone revealed that the Caillauxs, in December 1916, were staying at Hotel De Russie in Rome under the name of Reynouard. Reynouard was Madame Caillaux's maiden name.

* * * * * *

On January 14, 1918 Caillaux was placed under arrest for engaging in treasonable negotiations with the enemy. He was held in Sante Prison until September 1919. Then because of health reasons, he was transferred to a nursing home at Nevilly Sur Seine, but still under police detention.

His trial before the High Court of the Senate began on February 17, 1920. The war had ended on November 11, 1918, and the treaty of Versailles was signed in 1919. All of the Military Courts had been dismissed.

The Senate Trial in the Palais Du Luxembourg had no empty seats as Caillaux was brought into the Chamber. The High Court is a large semicircle facing a raised dais on which is the seat of the Oresident of the High Court, Leon Bourgeois. On his right, the public prosecutor Attorney Lescouve and the two Advocate Generals, one of who is former Lieutenant Andre Mornet of the Military Court, who was now dressed in the scarlet robe of a High Officer of Justice.

The accusations against Caillaux numbered six:

1. Conspiring with Bolo Pacha.

2. Supporting the policies of the *Bonnet Rouge*.

3. Dealing with the purchase of the paper *Le Journal* with German Funds.

4. His dealing with the Austro-Hungarian, Count Lipscher.

5. His relations with Count Minotto while in Buenos Aires and with the German minister Count Luxburg while there.

6. His visits to Italy and the contents of the Bank Deposit Vault he had in his wife's maiden name.

The relationship between Alphonse Lenoir, his son and Caillaux was unclear. Caillaux admitted that the father was one of his agents during the 1911 negotiations with Germany. However, he had no dealings with the son Pierre and the son's purchase of the newspaper *Le Journal*.

Pierre Lenoir was accused of using funds of German origin - $1.9 million to be exact – to purchase *Le Journal*. He was tried in 1917, convicted by the military court and executed.

The President of the High Court, Leon Bourgeois, began to question Caillaux on his relations with Lipscher, the Hungarian agent, and Madame Duverger.

Lipscher, as correspondent for the *Figaro*'s Budapest Office, offered Caillaux information for a price on Gaston Calmette and the Hungarian government. This information was to be used for the defense of Madame Caillaux. "He [Lipscher] brought me a weapon for the defense of my wife and my honor," Caillaux said. The documents showed that Hungarian Count Kalman Tisza had been subsidizing the *Figaro*.

During the war Lipscher was Agent to Baron Von Der Lancken, who at one time was councilor of the German Embassy in Paris. Madame Duverger, Lipscher's mistress, was a courier in carrying letters between Caillaux and Lipscher. The court wanted to know why the French Authorities weren't told that Foreign Agents were visiting him. He stated that he informed Prime Minister Briand. When Briand was called, he was asked if he was so informed of the Lipscher letters.

Briand replied, "I asked Viviani, the Minister of Defense, and Malvy, the Minister of the Interior, if they knew about the letters, they both replied no."

* * * * * *

The President of the Court opened his examination of Caillaux thus:

Question: "Was not Minotto's Mother a German?"

Answer: "I did not know it, nor did I know that he had been brought up in Germany. He came from London and said that he was intimate with the French and Italian ambassadors."

Question: "What were your relations with Count Luxburg?" [German Minister to Buenos Aires]

Answer: "Minotto told me the Count greatly admired me and would like to make my acquaintance. I replied, 'That is thoroughly German and just like their rudeness and treachery. At that time the German Press was very treacherous toward me. The *Neue Freie Presse* had published an article praising me, with the intention of damaging my position in France."

Question: How did the German Embassy obtain a copy of your report to French Minister of Commerce you sent from South America?

Answer: "I dictated the report to 'Little Minotto'. However, I am not the only person who was taken in by Minotto. When he came to France in 1915 he was introduced to the Governor of the Bank of France, not by me, and there given a mission. He was given information by the Governor of the Bank of France on the State of our finances."

The encounters between Minotto and Caillaux occurred in 1914 and 1915. The Count had the best of both worlds here in the United States. He had a "Title" and a high position in a Major New York Bank.

Until the United States entered the war in 1917, there were no restrictions on German Nationals. Minotto came to America in August 1914, arriving on the ship Campania. He and his two traveling companions, Count Von Zebeck and Fritz Kuhn, were all employed by one of the large German Banks in London. Count Von Zebeck changed his name to George Sebeck. Von Zebeck's father at the outbreak of the war commanded the German 10th Army Corp. Fritz Kuhn's father was the Director of a Bank in Mannheim ,Germany.

Because of their language skills and banking experience, they were all hired by the Guaranty Trust Company. They were, all three, friends of the Germany Ambassador Count Von Bernstorff and were guests many times at the summer embassy on Long Island in New York.

A European title in the United States at this period of time was an excellent way to increase your social standing in society. James Minotto claimed he was of Italian Nobility and was well accepted by the New York Social Set. In truth, his mother was a famous German actress and that he was born in Berlin.

In 1916, Ida May Swift, on a visit to New York, met Count Minotto, and after a short courtship they were married in a wedding ceremony at the Blackstone Hotel in Chicago. George Sebeck came to the wedding and acted as best man.

After the wedding, the Count and new Countess traveled to South America on their honeymoon, which also allowed Minotto to return to his duties as the bank representative. In April 1916, Secretary of the Treasury McAdoo and other members of the American Delegation visited Buenos Aires and were entertained by Count and Countess Minotto.

He was recalled from his second trip for his pro-German attitude. After his return from South America, he was transferred to the bond department. He then left the Guaranty Trust Company and was employed by the Equitable Trust Company. When it became apparent that the United States was going to enter the war, the Minottos moved to Chicago and the Count took employment with the Swift Meat Company.

In October 1917, when the Bolo Pacha affair was in the news, Mrs. Chauncey Eldridge of New York contacted the Justice Department with information linking Count Minotto with the Caillauxs in South America. Chauncey Eldridge, a radio engineer, was involved in building wireless stations in South America. They had social encounters with Minotto and also the Caillauxs while in Rio Janeiro.

C.H. Paul of the Immigration Department, called on the New York Police to arrest Fritz Kuhn and George Sebeck who were living at 12 Fifth Avenue New York City. On May 13, 1918, Count Minotto was arrested at the Lake Forest estate of his father-in-law, Louis Swift, on a Presidential Warrant, and brought before Judge George A. Carpenter of the United States District Court in Chicago. The ruling on Minotto followed the decision made on Kuhn and Sebeck. They were judged to be enemy agents and were sent to Fort Oglethorpe in Georgia for internment. The French authorities were also informed of the facts gathered concerning Minotto and Caillaux.

* * * * * *

The French Secret Service had a dossier on Caillaux and had a record of his travels to Italy, where the Caillauxs fled after Henriette's acquittal on the charge of murder. They were most interested in his trip to Rome in November 1916, where they stopped in Florence before going on to Rome. They were traveling under the name of Renovard, his wife's maiden name.

There they put a group of documents in a bank safe, and the French Secret Service now had those items. One group of papers was titled "Les Responsables – La Guece Et La Paix." The other group was called the "Rubicon."

The first papers were Caillaux's indictment of the French Political Leaders, "Those responsible for the war were not so much Germany and her leaders as the French Press and the French Government." The documents were all in the hand writing of Caillaux.

"Rubicon" was his outline for taking over the Government when Germany had defeated the French Army and the present Leaders were no longer in charge. He would change every Army Command. In the interior of the country, he would dismiss the Chamber of Deputies and bring certain army regiments into Paris. He proposed the arrest and prosecution of the direct and indirect authors of the war. He would legislate by decree and replace the usual constitutional government. He also outlined the steps to be taken as he became Prime Minister with the power to make peace.

* * * * * *

The final witness having been heard, it was now for the prosecution and the defense to present their closing speeches.

Attorney General Lescouve began his speech for the prosecution.

> *"In a conflict such as that we have just been through, there are three principles of a moral nature which dominate the conduct of the war. To conquer, one must first of all believe in victory. He must triumph who is determined never to yield, hence, the necessity of sustaining the ardor and confidence of the army and country. The second principle is that no one has the right to practice war policy other than that of the government which is alone responsible. The effect of negotiating mysterious conditions of peace outside the government is a plot against the security of the state. Finally, any aid given even indirectly to the enemy, political or economic, is a crime. The principles justify certain exceptions to the common law, such as censorship and postal control. Laws were voted against alarmist conversation and against commercial relations with the enemy. By the penal code, every maneuver, negotiation, or intelligence with the enemy is punishable."*

His complete closing speech lasted for three days.

The defense council, three in number, spent a comparable time with their closing speeches also. Defense Counsel Moutet was chosen to begin their closing arguments.

> *"In his long pitiless requistoire the Attorney General has accused Caillaux of having betrayed his country, and favored Germany's intrigues by seeking his ambition, Caillaux, according to the prosecution, was prepared to hesitate before nothing, even imposing himself by force and maintaining himself by violence. You have heard his conclusions. It is a political*

sentence which is asked of you. After this long trial it will be your opinion that no proof has been advanced and that the prosecution has been reduced to saying to us, prove your innocence."

"If you judge Caillaux guilty sentence him in tranquility, but if the crime of treason imputed to him appears to you imaginary, then I say to you – Liberty, Justice, Truth, that is France. The French patrimony is the noblest of all. Do not compromise it. Judge so that we may show that we have learned duty and justice."

In the course of their deliberating, the high court of justice, decided by a vote of 213 to 28 to reject the Attorney General's request to the application of articles 77 and 79 of the penal code (Intelligence with the Enemy). This would have entailed deportation to a fortified place for life.

The court next debated article 78 (Correspondence with the enemy), as a consequence of which Germany received information harmful to France and her allies. The penalty under article 78 is five to 20 years. This article 78 was approved by a vote of 150 to 91.

On April 23, 1920, the high court of justice delivered a verdict of guilty in the Caillaux case.

The accused is declared guilty of the crime which is punishable by article 78 of the penal code. Extenuating circumstances are admitted in favor of the accused. He is sentenced to three years imprisonment: to 10 years interdiction of rights of voting, eligibility or fitness for any public function: furthermore, five years prohibition to appear in certain places indicated by the government. Caillaux is also condemned to pay to the state the cost of the trial.

The verdict is based upon the following facts: The relations of Caillaux with Bolo and Almereyda did not fall under the penal code, but were retained as elements of morality. The constituents of the crime for which Caillaux had been sentenced were his close friendship with Minotto. It was ruled inadmissible that a former President of the Council, invested with an official mission, should have imparted his supposed grievances against the government and have thus given to Count Luxburg most harmful information on French Politics.

The facts proved against the accused are correspondence with agents of the enemy, with the result that information was furnished to the enemy contrary to the Military and political interest of France and her allies. This offense falls under article 78 of the penal code. Caillaux narrowly missed being sentenced to five years imprisonment, the voting on that issue 120 to 120.

Orders were given for the release of Caillaux from custody he had already served his sentence. He had been in custody for a period of 28 months, and it was the usual custom to allow a prisoner to benefit by the term he has already served in prison before his trial.

* * * * * *

One of the most unusual trials in the history of the French Republic came to its close.

To some the results were not surprising. One of those was Albert Sallie, Defense Counsel for Bolo. His question to the court in the defense of Bolo – "Why have this water tight justice? I know quite well that if Caillaux were here in the dock Bolo would be acquitted. Why is not Caillaux here? It is because of a desire to shield the man who was powerful yesterday and who may be powerful tomorrow, because the politicians desire to reserve for him a more comfortable fate before another court."

Epilogue

Joseph Caillaux was never far from his political friends, and in 1924, he was granted amnesty. In 1925 Caillaux was again Minister of Finance in the French Government, and was to get support to again become Prime Minister. Although he and his wife, Madame Caillaux, were hated by many people in France, his knowledge of government finances was needed and he made many important decisions from 1924 until his death in 1944. His wife preceded him in death in 1943.

Louis Malvy, like Caillaux, was convicted and banished from the country. He was sentenced to five years in exile. He returned from Spain in 1924 and he was again elected to serve in the National Assembly. Unlike Caillaux, Malvy never regained his prominence in the National Assembly. He died in 1949.

Captain Pierre Bouchardon became an examining magistrate after the war, and like other World War I veterans, he remained loyal to the government of Marshal Henri Petain. After the landings in Normandy by the British and Americans, and the invasions in Southern France, Bouchardon resigned from the Vichy government. After the war ended and Marshal Petain was arrested and charged with treason, Bouchardon was one of the investigators assigned to the case.

Lieutenant Andre Mornet had also served in the Vichy government, and like Bouchardon, decided to resign his position until the war was over. Lieutenant Mornet was appointed Procurator-General of the new French Government. He was the prosecutor in the Petain trial and demanded and got the death penalty for the old Marshal. The sentence was later commuted by Charles de Gaulle.

James Minotto, along with von Sebeck and Kuhn, were all decreed to be enemy agents of the U.S. – despite the best efforts of Louis Swift, his father-in-law – and were interned at Fort Oglethorpe, Georgia. They were released in January 1920. Minotto sailed for Europe in August 1920, but returned in 1921 and with the help of his wealthy father-in-law, he became a naturalized citizen. Who's Who in Chicago in 1926 has a listing on Minotto:

James Minotto, Vice President Boulevard Bridge Bank; Agent for Santa Catalina Island Company Wilmington Transportation, Arizona Board of Directors, Chicago Assoc. Of Commerce; Lake Shore Athletic Club;

Bankers Club of America

Homes: Lake Forest, Ill., Z. Triangle Ranch, Kirkland, Arizona

Count Johann Heinrich Bernstorff found himself at odds with the policies of Hitler and the National Socialists after the war, and he moved to Switzerland.

Characters & Chronology

Louis J. Malvy, Who as Minister Of
Interior, Failed to Suppress The Bolo Gang

Bolo Pacha, Now a Prisoner, Who Spent
Millions of German Money in France

Captain Pierre Bouchardon (*left*) and Lieutenant André Mornet, at or
shortly after Mata Hari's execution

M. Joseph Caillaux

2. Henriette Caillaux in a simple pose early in her marriage to Joseph Caillaux (*L'Illustration*, 21 March 1914).

Miguel Almereyda, editor of the *Bonnet Rouge*. This photograph of him was taken in his cell at *La Santé*, after the court had condemned him to three years of prison for insulting "the Fatherland and the Army" in 1909. *(Courtesy of the Hoover Institution on War, Revolution and Peace)*

Front page of the *Bonnet Rouge* for October 14, 1916. Note the blank spaces where articles have been heavily censored. The piece on the left ("Where Are the Pacifists?") has been drastically mutilated, and consists of an ironic attack on pacifists and pacifism, obviously designed to be read as a disguised statement of the newspaper's own pacifist position. *(Courtesy of the Hoover Institution on War, Revolution and Peace)*

Count Johann von Bernstorff, Imperial German Ambassador to the United States. His Machinations Continued until the Severance of Diplomatic Relations in 1917.

Captain Franz von Papen, Imperial German Military Attaché.

Louis Franklin Swift & Family
Husband of Ida May (Butler) Swift
(Ida was a granddaughter of Elizabeth Kalloch & Brackett Butler)

Louis F. Swift & (son-in-law) Count James Minotto - 1917
Standing in front of the United States Immigration Services General Offices

[Chicago Daily News negatives collection, DN-0069225 - Courtesy of the Chicago Historical Society]

Louis F. Swift's obituary

Louis' daughter, Ida May Swift
& horse Protection -1905
(age about 13)

[Chicago Daily News negatives collection, SDN-003729 -
Courtesy of the Chicago Historical Society]

Ida May Swift driving a horse-drawn carriag
Onwentsia Horse Show in Lake Forest, I
1905

[Chicago Daily News negatives collection, DN-0002813 - Co
Chicago Historical Society]

117993

FMO-JFD

January 8, 1918.

COPY FOR CHIEF OF BUREAU

A. B. Bielaski, Esq.,
Chief, Bureau of Investigation,
Department of Justice,
Washington, D. C.

Dear Sir:

Referring to your letter A. B. B. of
the 5th instant, received at this office yesterday, concerning information desired by Second
Deputy Attorney General Alfred L. Becker relative
to certain phases of the Bolo Pasha case, I beg
to advise that Agent Bielaski has made the necessary investigation, and I enclose herewith
photostat copies of certain messages, with information typewritten on the bottom of the message.

In addition to the information contained
in these notes, I beg to advise that the last
known address of J. O'Sullivan, 1021 Greenwood
Avenue, Richmond Hill, Long Island, where mail was
received by him as late as the 7th instant.

J. O'Sullivan, also referred to in some of
the notes on the bottom of these messages is now
employed on the night shift at the Postal Telegraph
Company, his true name being Christian, and his
residence address 89 Chichester Avenue, Jamaica,
Long Island.

The originals of these messages are on
file with the United States Naval Radio Station,
Sayville, Long Island, the name of the present cus-
todian of the records being W. R. Smith. The officer
in charge of the station at the time was Lieutenant
Commander C. B. Clark, United States Navy, whose
exact address cannot be furnished at this time, but

49

Chronology

M.I.4-35
June 27, 1918

SYNOPSIS

Marie-Paul Bolo
(Bolo Pacha)

(This synopsis is compiled chiefly from the depositions of A. Pavenstedt and others, taken by the Attorney General of New York for use in the Bolo trial; this material has been supplemented by information from M.I.B. files)

BIOGRAPHICAL NOTE

In his early twenties was a dentist at Marseille, then a colonial grocer, a lobster merchant and restaurant keeper. Ruined his partner and eloped with partner's wife to Spain. Five years later back in Paris and imprisoned for a month because of business dishonesty. Robbed neice of his hotel keeper at Hendays on Spanish frontier of her dowery. In 1893 in Bourdeaux, married his first wife, an actress. Arrested in Buenos Aires, and deserted his wife. In 1902, agent for champagne house at Lyons. In 1903 came to Paris. Married bigamously rich widow of Bordeaux wine merchant in 1905. Invested her money unsuccessfully principally in South America. Lived extravagantly in Paris. (9140-3977/15.)

Prior to 1914 became intimate with and financial adviser of Abbas Hilmi, Khedive of Egypt. Received title of Pacha. Attempted to form a Catholic Bank in which late Marquis Jules della Chiesa, brother of Pope Benedict and ex Khedive were to be interested. Plan not put through. (9140-3977/17).

ASSOCIATES.

Marie Louise Beragni
582 Lincoln Ave., Woodland Beach, Staten Island. French citizen, former employee of Mme. Buzenet. Knew Bolo, Lieutenant Verdier and Pavenstedt. Called Bolo several times by telephone for Lieut. Verdier.

Charles F. Bertelli
Paris, France.
French correspondent for Hearst papers. Made efforts to secure news exchange between Hearst papers and various French newspapers. Had large acquaintance with French publishers.

Mme. Marian Buzenet
Paris and New York City.
Came to United States with Perier on same steamer (La Fayette) with Bolo. Was member of firm, with Perier, of "Mme. Buzenet" importers of gowns and novelties. Left New York about March 6/16 for San Francisco with Perier.

Noureddin Flora
New York City.
Native of Albania, Valona. Lived in Switzerland in 1915. Met Bolo there in November at Lausanne. Connected by marriage with ex-Khedive Abbas Hilmi. Left Khedive in May 1916 after a quarrel about family matters. Knew of Bolo's dealings with Khedive and German agents, but did not participate in them.

Charles Humbert
Paris, France.
Senator - principal owner of Paris Journal. Born 1866. Humble parentage. Entered army at 18. Commissioned 2nd Lieut. some years later. Specialized in purchasing Department of Army. Acquired information on private affairs of influential men and used it for his own advancement. Entered Senate in 1908. Connected first with Journal 1909. Advocate of large artillery program 1914. After war began, accused of accepting money from Lenoir in Switzerland to buy into Journal. This money was part of

German plunder in invaded French territory. Later accused of taking German money from Bolo to enable him to continue control of Journal.

M. Panon
Paris.
Artist, had known Bolo since he was ten years old. Early business partner. Bolo ruined him financially and disappeared with his wife.

Adolph Pavenstedt
Born Hamburg, Germany 1854; came to United States 1876; spent 12 years in Cuba; also traveled in China, Japan and South America; unmarried. German subject. Partner in G. Amsinck & Co. 1901-16. Acted as intermediary between Bolo and Bernstorff in transferring funds. Close friend of Bernstorff. Interned Ft. Oglethorpe February 3, 1918.

Lieut. Paul Perier
Paris.
French officer. Proprietor of department store "City of Paris" in San Francisco. Attempted to start a branch in New York - venture failed after few months. Came to United States with Bolo. Note: Pavenstedt stated there was nothing in any conversations at which he was present to indicate that Verdier had any connection with Bolo's mission in U. S.

E. C. Pignatel.
645 West End Ave., New York.
Clerk for Royal Bank of Canada.

Justus Ruperti
New York City
Partner in G. Amsinck & Co. Later bought out A. Pavenstedt. Apparently never personally connected with Bolo's activities.

Hugo Schmidt
Ft. Oglethorpe, formerly 112 Central Park South, N. Y. C. German citizen. Took out first papers Feb. '16. Came to U. S. Oct. 1914 to act as agent for Deutsche Bank. Was authorized to give orders in name of Deutsche Bank to Guaranty Trust Co. Bankers Trust Co., Equitable Trust Co., Chase National Bank, Park National Bank, and Speyer & Co. Had similar authority with Mueller, Schall & Co. Knew A. Pavenstedt very well. Acted as paymaster, getting money from Berlin through Deutsche Bank for Bernstorff to pay to Bolo. Interned Jan. 21, 1918.

Mlle. Sonia Ouff
Last address 59th St., N.Y.C.
Came U. S. on Espagne shortly before Bolo and Perier. Was a model for Mme. Buzenet. Was intimate with Bolo while he was in U.S. Was later Pavenstedt's mistress until June 1917. Spent June to September 1916 in Paris.
Note: She was reported last to be in or near San Francisco, but no trace of her has been discovered.

Mme. Gabrielle Vergeade
Manager of "Mme. Buzenet", 714 Fifth Ave. came U.S. shortly before Bolo. Last address 56 Rue de la Pompe, Paris.

Chronology.

1914.

February   Bolo met A. Pavenstedt in Cuba

May   Bolo and M. Bauer, director of the Perier Bar.
Paris, visited J. P. Morgan & Co. to secure assistance in establishing bank in Cuba. Plan not
carried out. Morgan & Co. refused.

May   Bolo in New York. Staid probably ten days. Was
introduced by A. Pavenstedt to several N. Y. banks.
Came as agent for Perier Bank of Paris, to interest
U. S. capital in Cuban bank to be organized.

July   Bolo had spent wife's fortune. Was living on
her income from a trust fund. Income amounted to
about 8000 francs. (9140-3977/16)

August   A. Pavenstedt wrote Henri Bauer, of Perier
Bank, expressing regret that war had been declared.
G. Amsinck & Co. were correspondents of Perier Bank.

1915.

Bolo and Khedive met in Switzerland. Von Jagow
provided 10,000,000 marks to be used by Bolo to
influence French press for premature peace.

April   Cavallini took $400,000 to Bolo in Paris, to
be used for "defeatist" and pacifist propaganda.
Bolo claimed this was repayment of loan made to
Khedive.

November and December   Bolo met Khedive in Lausanne, Switzerland.
Also negotiated through Khedive with several Ger-
man agents there. Abbas Hilmi stated that Bolo represented Gustav Herve, publisher of La Victoire,
and Joseph Caillaux and others; that Bolo was to
receive money from German officials at this time
and deliver it to Herve and Caillaux in France.
Khedive gave Bolo 2,000,000 marks which Khedive received from Germany.
Note: This money was to be used to pay "the newspaper (Journal) and these political people like
Caillaux and Herve". The purpose of these negotiations was to secure a separate peace with France
for Germany.

1916.

February 5   H. Bauer of Perier & Co. Paris, wrote letter
of introduction for Bolo to R. H. Jones, agent in
N.Y. for Royal Bank of Canada. "...Bolo Pacha who
is going to the U.S.A. on a mission touching high
personalities of your country."

May

       Bolo in New York. Staid probably ten days. Was introduced by A. Pavenstedt to several N. Y. banks. Came as agent for Perier Bank of Paris, to interest U. S. capital in Cuban bank to be organized.

July

       Bolo had spent wife's fortune. Was living on her income from a trust fund. Income amounted to about 8000 francs. (9140-3977/16)

August

       A. Pavenstedt wrote Henri Bauer, of Perier Bank, expressing regret that war had been declared. G. Amsinck & Co. were correspondents of Porier Bank.

       1915.

       Bolo and Khedive met in Switzerland. Von Jagow provided 10,000,000 marks to be used by Bolo to influence French press for premature peace.

April

       Cavallini took $400,000 to Bolo in Paris, to be used for "defeatist" and pacifist propaganda. Bolo claimed this was repayment of loan made to Khedive.

November and December

       Bolo met Khedive in Lausanne, Switzerland. Also negotiated through Khedive with several German agents there. Abbas Hilmi stated that Bolo represented Gustav Herve, publisher of La Victoire, and Joseph Caillaux and others; that Bolo was to receive money from German officials at this time and deliver it to Herve and Caillaux in France. Khedive gave Bolo 2,000,000 marks which Khedive received from Germany.
Note: This money was to be used to pay "the newspaper (Journal) and those political people like Caillaux and Herve". The purpose of these negotiations was to secure a separate peace with France for Germany.

       1916.

February 5

       H. Bauer of Perier & Co. Paris, wrote letter of introduction for Bolo to R. Z. Jones, agent in N.Y. for Royal Bank of Canada. "...Bolo Pacha who is going to the U.S. on a mission touching high personalities of your country."

February 10

       Humbert wrote J. P. Morgan & Co. that Bolo would deposit 1,000,000 francs with Morgan to Humbert's account.

February 10

       Note: This letter is at variance with Pavenstedt's whole story which is in substance that Bolo landed in N.Y. on Feb. 22, practically without funds and desperately in need of money to buy the Journal stock from Humbert; and that the transaction had not been planned in advance. Pavenstedt's only explanation was that Bolo was very vain and self confident and had told Humbert that he could get the money at once in U. S.; that Humbert's letter reflected Bolo's confidence.

February 22

       Charles F. Bertelli and Lieut. Verdier landed New York with Bolo on S. S. La Fayette.

New York with Bolo on S. S. La Fayette.

February 22   Bolo arrived New York met Adolph Pavenstedt at
Plaza Hotel night of his arrival. A confidential
letter arrived at the same time from Perier & Co.,
Bolo's Paris bankers, limiting his credit with
G. Amsinck & Co. to $2500.
Note: This would confirm statement that Bolo at
this time was without large resources. At first
interview Bolo said he was in financial difficulties
and needed money; gave Pavenstedt a contract between
Bolo and Humbert to read.

February 23   Pavenstedt returned contract to Bolo. This
contract provided that Humbert had sold a very large
interest in Le Journal to Bolo, stated how profits
were to be divided, and stipulated that Humbert was
to retain control of editorial columns and dictate
the "tone" or policy of paper.
Bolo explained that he had not paid for his
interest and had come to U. S. to get financial assistance. Also stated he wanted to get money to
buy interest in several small papers, in addition
to paying debt to Humbert.

February 23   Pavenstedt first discussed with Bolo the securing of money from Bernstorff.

February 24   Shoreham Hotel register shows Pavenstedt reg-
istered there that day.

February 24   Jones, New York Agent, Royal Bank of Canada,
wrote Bauer that he would assist Bolo in obtaining
print paper.

February 24   Jones, N. Y. agent, wrote and wired C. E. Neill,
General Manager, Royal Bank of Canada, asking if
Canadian paper mill could supply large quantity of
paper for Bolo who was to purchase paper for Journal
and other French papers.

February 24   F. F. Walker, Royal Bank of Canada, wrote Jones,
agent in N. Y. that Canadian mills could supply
paper provided payment was made on delivery at American or Canadian ports.

February   Bertelli introduced Bolo to Hearst.

February   Hearst invited Bolo and Bertelli to lunch soon
after Bolo's arrival in U.S.; at luncheon, Hearst
said he was pro-French in sentiment.

February 25!   Interview Bolo and Pavenstedt. Bolo wanted
10,000,000 francs and offered his shares in Journal
as collateral. Pavenstedt said he could not consider
it as a business proposition. Bolo then said object
of his loan was to bring French public opinion
around to desire for early peace; that France was

bleeding to death; that Humbert was his partner in the matter. Bolo proposed to keep the securities in a Paris bank and to pay no interest on the loan. Idea was that some one in America from sentimental reasons might advance the money in hope of ending war. Ford's name suggested.

Perier & Co. did not know Bolo's plans but supposed he was going to U.S. to buy print paper.

February 25?
Pavenstedt told Bolo: "I only know one man who might be interested in your proposition and that is Count Bernstorff. Would you have any objection to my speaking to him." Bolo replied: "You do whatever you think, I leave that to you."

February 26
Bernstorff cabled von Jagow that "a political action in one of the enemy countries....will bring peace." "Leading political personality of the country is seeking a loan of one million seven hundred thousand dollars in New York. Can the money be provided at once in New York?"

February 26?
Pavenstedt submitted proposition to Bernstorff in Washington. Bernstorff was interested; said it would be desirable to change feeling of French people to favor early peace.

February 26?
Bolo had lunch with Mr. Vorhees, formerly with Royal Bank of Canada and later with National City Bank. Bolo did not ask Voorhees to finance his scheme.

February 27?
Pavenstedt returned to New York and told Bolo of interview with Bernstorff.

February 29
Von Jagow cabled Bernstorff: "Agree to loan but only if peace action seems to you a really serious project as the provision of money in New York is for us at present extraordinarily difficult." Cable also says: "If Russia or Italy is meant, nothing is to be done as amount is too small to affect Russia, and Italy would not justify so large an expenditure."

March 2?
Bernstorff met Pavenstedt in N.Y. at Ritz. Told Pavenstedt that he would advance the money. P. wrote note to Bolo that money would be forthcoming. Saw Bolo later same day at Plaza. Bolo wrote a longhand memorandum addressed to Pavenstedt stating that money would be repaid two years after the war. That the securities - shares of Journal stock - would be deposited in a Paris bank in Pavenstedt's name. Pavenstedt assumed no personal responsiblity and acted merely as agent for German Ambassador. Bolo's name not given to Bernstorff by Pavenstedt.

Bernstorff told Pavenstedt that Hugo Schmidt would furnish the money. Bolo told P. to place money to his account with Royal Bank of Canada. Pavenstedt told Schmidt to pay the money in smaller amounts over period of three weeks and to make checks to G. Amsinck & Co. Schmidt replied that money would be paid through Guarantee Trust Co. and National Park Bank.

March 4
Pavenstedt had conference with Bernstorff at which Bernstorff said he would provide the money.

55

March 4   Bolo wrote note from Hotel Plaza to J.P. Morgan
                       saying the credit in favor of Humbert would be es-
                       tablished.
                       Note: This is two days before Schmidt's first wire-
                       less to Deutsche Bank asking for funds. This is
                       also evidence that the matter had been arranged be-
                       fore Bolo arrived in U. S.

March 5   Bernstorff cabled von Jagow: "Please instruct
                       Deutsche Bank to hold nine million marks at dis-
                       posal of Hugo Schmidt. The affair is very promising."

March 6   Letter to G. Amsinck & Co. from Bolo.
                       "You will receive for my account sums of mon-
                       ey of which A. Pavenstedt knows the amount. Will
                       you be good enough to apply them to the credit of
                       my account at the New York Branch of the Royal Bank
                       of Canada?"

                       The Hugo Schmidt - Deutsche Bank Wireless mess-
                       ages.
                       Note: It seems fairly clear from Pavenstedt's test-
                       imony that the German money used in this transact-
                       ion was physically in America at the time and the
                       following wireless messages from Berlin merely au-
                       thorized Schmidt to transfer the necessary amount
                       for the particular purpose.

March 6   Hugo Schmidt to Deutsche Bank: "Communicate
                       Auswart Amt. (foreign office)
                       with William Pexiey and telegraph whether he has
                                                               Count
                       placed money at my disposal with you for Charles-
                       Bernstorff.
                       Gledhill."

March 12   Deutsche Bank to Hugo Schmidt: "Replying your
                                 Count Bernstorff Guarantee Trust Co.
                       cable about Charles-Gledhill Fred-Heeven will re-
                       ceive money for our account you may dispose accord-
                                                       Guarantee Trust Co.
                       ing our letter Nov. 24th 1914 to Fred-Heeven."

March 14   Hugo Schmidt to Deutsche Bank: "Your wireless
                                 Count Bernstorff 500,000
                       received paid Charles-Gledhill-five-hundred dollars
                                 Guarantee Trust Co. Bernstorff
                       through Fred-Heeven. Gledhill requires further
                       1,100,000
                       eleven-hundred dollars which shall pay gradually."

March 17   Deutsche Bank to Schmidt: "You may dispose
                       Guarantee Trust Co. Count Bernstorff 1,700,000
                       on Fred-Heeven on behalf Charles-Gledhill-seventeen
                       thousand dollars."

                                                               Count Bernstorff
March 18   Schmidt to Deutsche Bank: "Paid Charles-Gledhill
                                 300,000
                       further three-hundred."

                                                               Count Bernstorff
March 24   Schmidt to Deutsche Bank: "Paid Charles-Gledhill
                                 200,000
                       further two-hundred-dollars."

56

April 1

Schmidt to Deutsche Bank. "Paid Charles-Gledhill 483,500 four-hundred-eighty-three-a-half dollars as final payment."

Note: The foregoing messages are set out serially, without regard to chronology of other events, to give connected story of this phase of the case.

March 6

Bolo wrote from Plaza to Royal Bank directing it to place with J. P. Morgan & Co. a credit of 1,000,000 francs for Humbert and charge same to Bolo's account.

March 6 ?

Bernstorff requests Schmidt to meet him at Hotel Ritz, N. Y. Told Schmidt to cable Berlin for $1,700,000. Said he (B) had already cabled German foreign office.

Note: Schmidt claimed he did not know what the money was to be used for. Bernstorff told Schmidt to place this money at A. Pavenstedt's disposal when it came.

Note: In Sept. '17 Pavenstedt told Schmidt what the money had been used for.

March 7?

Bolo was introduced to Pignatel by R. E. Jones, agent of the Royal Bank of Canada. Bolo wanted to buy print paper, and Pignatel took him to International Paper Co. office at 30 Broad St., N.Y. No purchase made.

Note: It is probable that this conversation took place ten days prior to date given, as evidence is clear that Bolo discussed the print paper proposition before his negotiations with Bernstorff began.

Note: Below appears the exchange of the money, secured by the preceding wireless messages, between the several banking institutions.

March 13 — $500,000 passed from Guarantee Trust Co.
through G. Amsinck & Co. to
Royal Bank of Canada for acct. of
Bolo.
March 17 — 200,000 " " " " "
March 21 — 300,000 passed from National Park Bank
for acct. of Bolo
March 25 — 200,000 " " " Guar. Trust Co.
April 1 — 200,000 " " " "
April 1 — 283,500 " " " Nat. Park Bank
1,683,500

Note: (The above money came to Guarantee Trust Co. and National Park Bank for the account of the Deutsche Bank of Berlin by order of Hugo Schmidt.)

March 14

Bolo wrote Royal Bank giving following disposition of the total deposit: $170,068.03 to J. P. Morgan & Co. to credit of Senate Charles Humbert; $506,045.70 to Agency "T" of Comptoir National d' Escompte de Paris for credit Madame Bolo; $1,000,00 to J. P. Morgan and Co. for credit of Bolo; a few small amounts, including $5000 to Jules Bois.

March

Hearst dinner — given in N.Y. by Bolo at Cherry's one hundred and twenty five people present. Present: Mme. Buzenet, W. R. Hearst and wife, Adolph Pavenstedt, Captain Perier, Bolo Pacha, Mr. and Mrs.

Julian Gerard (brother of James W. Gerard) Jules
Bois (French poet, sent officially to lecture in U.S.)
Mr. Van Anda, managing editor N.Y. Times, Mrs. Owen
Johnson, Chas. F. Bertelli.
(Pavenstedt says there were 12 people at this dinner.

March   W. R. Hearst gave theatre party and supper
for Bolo after Bolo's dinner. Among guests were
Judge Gary, of U.S. Steel Corporation and Mr. and Mr
Sweeney.

March ?   George Kessler of N.Y. was introduced to Bolo
by Edmond Pavenstedt of Mueller Schall & Co. a sus-
pected firm. (9140-3977/12).
Note: This is the only mention which has been
found of E. Pavenstedt with Bolo.

March 15?   Bolo told Pignatel that reason he was drawing
such large sums from G. Amsinck & Co. and putting
them with Royal Bank, was that Amsinck had been loan-
ing his money for him in South America at high interests, but that he (Bolo) thought the firm was
pro-German and consequently wanted to take his account away. Told Pignatel he owned Paris Journal.

March   Bolo invested 1,000,000 francs in Journal, but
agreed to leave editorial policy in Humbert's hands.
Bolo made several attempts to get a laudatory article about American newspaper man in Journal. Finally succeeded when "excessive praise" had been e-
liminated.
Note: This doubtless refers to Hearst.

March 20   Bernstorff cabled von Jagow "Advise our Minister in Berne that some one will call on him who will
give him the password 'Saint Regis' and who wishes
to establish relations with the foreign office. Intermediary further requests that influence may be
brought to bear upon our press to pass over the
change in the inner political situation in France so
far as possible in silence, in order that things
may not be spoiled by German approval."
Note: Pavenstedt says this was done at Bolo's request, so he could be received by the German officials in Switzerland, if necessary.

Spring   Note: At this time Bolo's activities were
most open. Bolo, Caillaux, several members of the
French Chamber of Deputies and several French newspapers were engaged in an effort to spread propaganda that France could not win the war, and that
an early peace should be concluded.

April?   Bertelli made repeated attempts to get lauda-
May ?   tory articles on Hearst into Journal. Articles re-
June   fused by French Postal Censor because Hearst con-
sidered pro-German.

April ?   La Victoire printed eulogy of Hearst; also
May ?   described Bolo's relations with American press.

May 3   Laudatory article on W. R. Hearst appeared in
Paris Journal signed M. Meuthon. Prepared by Bolo.

Spring

    W. R. Hearst's mother stopped giving him finan-cial assistance. Paper makers were about to sue him. Could only obtain paper by sending check with order. Later Hearst was in shape to make prompt payments. Hearst papers have been pro-German. Suspected that Bolo may have bought quantities of paper and arrange for its delivery to Hearst in return for pro-German activities of Hearst papers. (9140-3977/34).
Note: There is no evidence found in this office substantiating this suspicion.

May ?

    Humbert, Bolo, Mouthon, editor of Journal, and Bertelli met and discussed exchange of news be-tween Journal and Hearst papers. Plan not consum-mated. (9140-3977/19).

May 31

    Von Jagow cabled Bernstorff: "The person an-nounced in telegram 692 of March 20th, has not yet reported himself at the legation in Berne. Is there any more news on your side of Bolo?"
Note: Pavenstedt unable to explain how von Jagow secured Bolo's name.

June 10

    J. P. Morgan & Co. transferred $1,000,000 to N.Y. Agency Royal Bank of Canada for account of Per-ier Co., Paris.

July 1

    A. Pavenstedt sold out his interest in G. Amsin-ck and Co. to Justus Ruperti.

December

    Caillaux went to Rome. Briand authorized Ital-ian Government to expell Caillaux. Action not taken. Caillaux attempted negotiations with Italian offi-cials for peace with Germany by France and Italy in spring of 1917. Also saw several pacifist cardin-als at Vatican. (10581-7/3).

1917.

Feb. 14

    When Bernstorff left U. S., Pavenstedt for first time told him that Bolo had been the man to whom the money was paid in March 1916.

March

    Bolo sent W. Panon to N. Y. to secure from A. Pavenstedt and Amsinck Bank statement of Bolo's ac-count from May 1914 to February 1917. Bolo asked Panon to have Amsinck & Co. cable as follows: "We send your account from the first transfer in May, 1914, of $1,500,000 or $1,700,000 to the transfers of February 1916 to the Royal Bank of Canada for the creation of a Cuban Bank." Pavenstedt told Panon this cable could not be sent.
Note: This was an obvious effort on Bolo's part to "fix" a record of his money transactions in U. S. which would appear to show that he had money in U.S. prior to getting the funds from Bernstorff in Feb-ruary 1916).

April

    Bolo met Bertelli and stated that he had been charged with treason.

September ?

    Bertelli offered to repay money previously borrowed from Bolo, when Bolo was accused.

September	Paul Painlere, Minister of War, turned over documents bearing on Bolo case which had been in his possession since April, 1917.
October 31	George Amsinck & Co. reported as having sold out to America International Corporation.(9140-3977/?

1918.

January 14	Joseph Caillaux, ex premier, arrested.
Feb. 4	Bolo trial opened in Paris. Charge: communicating with enemy in Switzerland and Paris in 1915; receiving German money to further pacifist movement; receiving money in U. S. in February and March 1916 to influence French newspapers, particularly Journal.
February 5	Bolo testified that in 1916 Pavenstedt professed to be a Czech and to hate Germany; that Pavenstedt never mentioned Bernstorff's name.
February 6	Bolo testified that his pre-war fortune of 2,000,000 francs made an 8,000,000 franc profit in two years because it was invested in war stocks in U.S. He had no books, records or other papers showing his financial transactions, or his claimed transfer of his money from Deutsche Bank to Amsinck & Co. in 1915. Note: Other evidence herein indicates Bolo was practically without resources when war started in 1914.
February 7	Charles Humbert testified in Bolo trial. Suspected as possible conspirator with Bolo to use Journal's influence to bring about peace.
February 9	Chas. F. Bertelli, head of Paris Bureau, International news service, testified that Bolo spoke patriotically on his trip to U. S. in 1916.
February 14	Bolo condemned to death. Filippo Cavallinie, a co-defendant, sentenced to death by default. In prison in Italy at time sentenced; could not be extradited.
February	Joseph Caillaux, ex French Premier, arrested, charged with treason in connection with Bolo.
February 23	Monseigneur Bolo, a Catholic Priest and brother of Bolo Pacha, wrote Mme. Blanche Henrion asking her if her American friends could prove that cablegrams between Bernstorff and Jagow were forged. Mme. Henrion wrote Mrs. Eugene Claudet, 145 Woodland Ave., New Rochelle, N.Y. who replied that she considered Bolo guilty, and would do nothing.
March 1	Painleve, ex Prime Minister of France, makes written explanation and defense of his failure to furnish certain documentary evidence (Casella report) to the authorities prosecuting Bolo. The information was withheld from April to September, 1917. Note: Explanation not clear, but apparently one copy should have been sent immediately to the proper authorities and Painleve did not know until September that it had not been.
March 19	Captain George J. Ladoux, Chief Intelligence Bureau, ordered tried on charge of trading with enemy and sedition in connection with Bolo Pacha.

Appendix A: The Money Trail

```
Before

    THE ATTORNEY GENERAL

        OF THE STATE OF NEW YORK.
...........................................

        IN  THE  MATTER
           -of the-

Inquiry as to MARIE PAUL BOLO,
otherwise known as PAUL BOLO PACHA.

...........................................

...........................................

        IN  THE  MATTER
           -of the-

Examinations into the financial
transactions of MARIE PAUL BOLO,
otherwise known as PAUL BOLO PACHA,
conformatory to the Rogatory Commis-
sion issued by Captain Bouchardon in
charge of reports to the Third Per-
manent Court Martial of the Military
Government of Paris, dated the 15th
day of June 1917, as supplemented
by the Rogatory Commission issued
by the said Captain Bouchardon,
dated as aforesaid, the 5th day of
October 1917.

...........................................
```

Murray Hill Hotel, New York City,
November 22nd, 1917, 2 o'clock P.M.

A D O L F   P A V E N S T E D T, called as a witness pur-

suant to a subpoena issued by the Attorney-General of

the State of New York and served personally upon him

STATE OF NEW YORK
OFFICE OF THE ATTORNEY-GENERAL
ALBANY

MERTON E. LEWIS
ATTORNEY-GENERAL
ALFRED L. BECKER
SECOND DEPUTY

PRESS ALL COMMUNICATIONS TO
ATTORNEY GENERAL

Murray Hill Hotel,
December 29, 1917.

Hon. John Lord O'Brian,
    Special Assistant to the Attorney General,
        Washington, D. C.

My dear John:

        The French Ambassador has requested us to
perfect somewhat the proof in the Bolo case.   The French
authorities would like to have proof of the actual sending
and receipt of the wireless messages. I take it that the
primary evidence in this case is the record of the wireless
station at Sayville. I am annexing transcripts of the messages involved and will thank you to communicate with the
proper authorities and ascertain:

        1-   The name of the operator who received and trans-
    mitted each of such messages and his present address, if
    available.

        2-   The name of the custodian of the records of such
    messages and his present address, if available.

        3-   The names of the naval officers in charge of the
    censorship of the Sayville station at the time of these
    messages, and their present addresses.

        4-   Where the original record books of messages of
    these dates now are.

        It is by no means certain that I shall be able to
furnish the French Ambassador all of the evidence that he wants
as a good part of it may be outside of the State of New York.
However, if I can obtain the above information I shall be able
to arrange to inform him so that he can make other arrangements
if necessary.

        The Ambassador is rather in haste to receive this
proof, so I respectfully request that you give it priority to
other matters.

        With best wishes for the New Year, I am, as ever
                Sincerely yours,

                            Second Deputy Attorney General

62

MR. BECKER: The stenographer will copy the letter
in the record.

"Berlin, den 15. M a r z 1916.

(Stamped: RECEIVED
Apr 17 1916
Answered............
By ....)

M.

Herrn

Direktor Hugo S c h m i d t

N e w Y o r k.

Wir bestatigen unseren depeschenwechsel, worin wir Ihnen Mit-
(in pencil:Guaranty Trust Co)   (in pencil:Reichsbank)
teilten, dass Fred Hooven auf Veranlassung von Fred Dole

$17,000.00   (In pencil: $1,700,000)

(vgl. in Ihrem Schreiben No.1357 die letzte Zeile)

fur unsere Rechnung erhalten wird. (in ink: auf der ersten
                                                          Zeile)
    Zu gleicher Zeit Benachrichtigen wir Sie, dass Sie dagegen
                                 (In pencil:Count Bernstorff)
den Gleichen Betrag zur Vorfugung des Herrn Charles Gladhill
halten mogen und erhielten wir hierauf bereits heute Ihr draht-
loses Telegramm, wonach Sie an den genannten Herrn

$5000.00   (In pencil: $500,000.-)

zur Auszehlung gebracht haben; wir nahmen weiter davon Kennt-
nis, dass der genannte Herr noch uber einen weiteren Betrag von

$11,000   (In pencil: $1,100,000)

zu verfugen gedenke.

    Wir begrussen Sie
                              freundschaftlichst
                        (Signed) Lubarsch ----- Hermann.

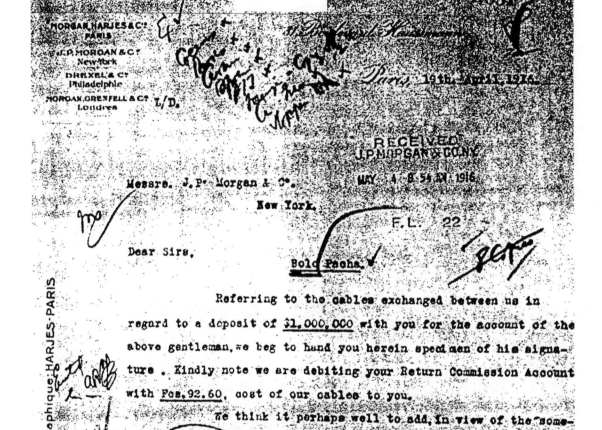

MORGAN HARJES & C°
PARIS

J.P. MORGAN & C°
New York

DREXEL & C°
Philadelphie

MORGAN, GRENFELL & C°
Londres

L/D.

Paris 19th April 1916

RECEIVED
J.P. MORGAN & C° N.Y.
MAY 4 8 54 AM 1916

Messrs. J. P. Morgan & C°.
New York.

F. L. 22

Dear Sirs,

Bolo Pacha.

Referring to the cables exchanged between us in regard to a deposit of $1,000,000 with you for the account of the above gentleman, we beg to hand you herein specimen of his signature. Kindly note we are debiting your Return Commission Account with Fcs. 92.60, cost of our cables to you.

We think it perhaps well to add, in view of the somewhat oriental sohance of this gentleman's name and title, that he is not a Turk, and in fact is the brother of a well known French Archbishop.

Yours very truly,
PP MORGAN HARJES & C°

EXHIBIT "O" - Concluded 2.

PHOTOGRAPHIC COPY OF STUB FROM CHECK BOOK OF G. AMSINCK & CO.

APR 3 - 1916   43702

Royal Bank of Canada

exchanged

413500

APR 3 - 1916   43703

PHOTOGRAPHIC COPY OF RECEIPT OF THE ROYAL BANK OF CANADA TO G. AMSINCK & CO.

New York   APR 3 - 1916   191

Received from Messrs. G. Amsinck & Co.

by order of   Mr. Paul Bolo Pacha

and for account   ORIGINAL   Dollars

THE ROYAL BANK OF CANADA
NEW YORK CITY

(Trans.F.A.) F.L.23/1126
Rec.Mar.5,1917

1616

Paris, February 7, 1917.

Messrs. J.P.Morgan & Co.,
23 Wall Street,
New York.

Gentlemen:-

I have not received the interest statement of my account in your Bank, and, consequently, do not have sufficient data to make up my declaration relative to the Income Tax conformably to the American law.

I therefore ask you to kindly make out same in my name and I herewith append the necessary information:

Name:	- Humbert
Christian Name	- Charles
Occupation	- Senateur de la Meuse and Manager of the paper "LE JOURNAL"
Address	- Paris, 167 Boulevard Malesherbes.
Husband of	- Nathan Marie

Madame Humbert has no personal income from American source.

Besides my account in your Bank, I own the American securities enumerated below:

14 (fourteen) New York Telephone 4½ Bonds, £100 denomination

3 (three)   New York Telephone 4½ Bonds, £200 denomination

10 (Ten)   Louisville & Nashville RR.4% $1000. Bonds

Please accept, Gentlemen, the expression of my most distinguished sentiments.

C. Humbert.

Appendix A

RECEIVED AND TRANSMITTED VIA SAYVILLE.

No. 1.

Deutsche Bank Direction, Berlin.
Communicate with with William Foxley and telegraph
whether he has placed money at my disposal with you
for Charles Gledhill.

March 6, 1916.   Hugo Schmidt.

No. 2.   Wireless from Deutsche Bank, Berlin, received
March 13, 1916, as follows: Replying your cable about
Charles Grehill stop Fred Hooven will receive money for
our account.You may disburse according our letters
November 24, 1914, to Fred Hooven.

No. 3.   Deutsche Bank Direktion, Berlin.
Your wireless received. Paid Charles Gledhill five
hundred dollars through Fred Hooven stop Gledhill
requires further eleven hundred dollars which shall
pay gradually
March 13, 1916.   Hugo Schmidt.

No. 4.   Wireless from Deutsche Bank, Berlin, received
March 17, 1916. You may disburse on Fred Hooven on
behalf Charles Gledhill seventeen thousand dollars.

No. 5.   Deutsche Bank, Direktion, Berlin.
Have received all details about City bonds stop
Paid Charles Gledhill further two hundred dollars.
March 19, 1916.   Hugo Schmidt.

No. 6.   Deutsche Bank Direktion, Berlin.
Paid Charles Gledhill further three hundred.
March 20, 1916.
                                                  Hugo Schmidt.

No. 7.   Deutsche Bank Direktion, Berlin.
Drafts Langman now arrived shall I discount stop
Discounted 1780 dollars Henshaw bills at two seven
eighths Paid Charlest Gledhill further two hundred
dollars
March 24, 1916.   Hugo Schmidt.

No. 8.   Deutsche Bank Direktion
Paid Charles Gledhill four hundred eighty three and
half dollars as final payment stop All your offers arrived too late Renew only offer Japanese.
April 1, 1916.   Hugo Schmidt.

Appendix A

#8990

January 10, 1918.

Paul Pasha Bolo.
Residence Unknown.

J. P. Morgan & Company, New York City, reports
a bank account of $259.95, as belonging to the above
party.

Appendix A

PERLEY MORSE & COMPANY
CERTIFIED PUBLIC ACCOUNTANTS
SIXTY-ONE BROADWAY
NEW YORK
TELEPHONE 1083 1084 RECTOR
CABLE ADDRESS "STANDIT"

December 29, 1917.

Hon. Lee S. Overman, United States Senator,
Chairman, Committee on Rules,
   United States Senate,
     Washington, D. C.

My dear Senator Overman:-

     You will no doubt remember me as the Accountant for James Phillips, Jr., Esq. Assuming that you have had and now have a great many things on your mind, I state the above to recall myself definitely to your recollection.

     Recently my organization, composed of one hundred, more or less, trained expert Accountants, was retained by Hon. Merton E. Lewis, Attorney General of the State of New York through His Excellency, the Governor of the State of New York to investigate the activities of Bolo Pacha in the United States for the French Ambassador, M. J. J. Jusserand. Our investigation disclosed generally the following:-

    1 - That Bolo Pacha received in this country through German sources about Two Million ($2,000,000.00) Dollars which was transmitted to France to buy up the French press in the interest of German propaganda in that country. Our reports in connection with this are very complete, containing photographs of all respective financial transactions in the books of the banks and individuals handling these funds.

    2 - The disclosure of the beginning of other financial transactions involving the German Government through bank accounts carried by the Deutsch Bank, the Reichs Bank and other German banks. For instance it was disclosed that the Deutsch Bank carried accounts with the Guaranty Trust Company, the National Park Bank, Bankers Trust Company, National City Bank, Equitable Trust Company, Chase National Bank, James Speyer & Co., etc.; that the Reichs Bank carried accounts with Kuhn, Loeb & Co. and the Riggs National Bank; and that Count von Bernstorff carried accounts with the Corn Exchange Bank.

     I have in my possession transcripts and photographs of the bank accounts of almost all of the above. These photographs disclose the names of individuals, firms, banks, corporations, etc. here in New York and throughout the country who have paid money or securities to, or received money or securities from these accounts.

DIRECTION

Paris, le 7 Février 1913

Pour le compte de: Madame Marie.

Messieurs J. P. Morgan & Cie.
23 Wall Street,

New York.

Messieurs,

Madame Humbert n'a pas de revenus personnels de source américaine.

En dehors de mon compte à votre Banque, je possède les valeurs américaines ci-après énumérées:

14 (Quatorze) Obligations New York Téléphone 4 1/2, coupures de 100 $

3 (Trois) Obligations New York Téléphone 4 1/2, coupures de 200 $

10 (Dix) Obligations Chemin de Fer Louisville and Nashville Rail Road (4 %) de Mille dollars

Je n'ai pas reçu le décompte des intérêts de mon dépôt à votre Banque et, par suite, je n'ai pas les éléments suffisants pour établir ma déclaration relative à l'impôt sur le revenu conformément à la Loi américaine.

Je vous prie donc de bien vouloir le faire en mon nom et je vous donne ci-après les renseignements nécessaires:

Nom: Humbert

Prénom: Charles

Veuillez agréer, Messieurs, l'expression de mes sentiments les plus distingués.

Appendix B: Newspaper Stories About Bolo Pacha

BOLO'S CAREER.

AN ADVENTURER IN TWO HEMISPHERES.

SOCIAL AND FINANCIAL FORTUNES.

(FROM OUR OWN CORRESPONDENT.)

PARIS, FEB. 5.

The indictment read by Captain Bouchardon in yesterday's proceedings at the Bolo trial gives a wonderful picture of the life of the adventurer. He is first of all shown as being a wideawake person, who even at school knew what life was and how to get the best of it. His brother, who is now a popular and respected preacher of the Roman Catholic Church in Paris, and a Monsignor to boot, said of him when Paul was at school "He is extremely intelligent, but he frightens me."

Captain Bouchardon gives the following portrait of Bolo when he was 19 years old:—

At that age he made his first entry into life. Physically he was possessed of advantages of which he well knew the value. He was blond, tall, slim, elegant in figure, had a silken moustache, a fondling eye, an inexhaustible source of fun, and was a master of cajolery with all the ways of a conqueror, a flirt and a feline philanderer—such was Bolo.

With all these natural gifts Bolo at an early age became a dentist at Marseilles. He then successively became a colonial grocer, a lobster merchant, and a restaurant keeper. In these undertakings he ruined his partner, and ran off with his partner's wife to Spain. Five years afterwards he was back in Paris, running a vague business which eventually ended in his getting a sentence of a month's imprisonment. The next trace of him is at Hendaye, on the Spanish frontier, where, according to the indictment, he robbed the niece of his hotel-keeper of her dowry. In 1893 he is found at Bordeaux. There he made the acquaintance of his first wife, who is among the witnesses—Mlle. Soumaille—conquered her with his silken moustaches and fondling eye, and vanished with her to Buenos Aires, where she played at a music hall. It was at that time that the prisoner called himself by, in fact signed his wife's contract with, the name of Bolo de Grange-Neuve. Shortly afterwards he was arrested at Valparaiso, and his wife gave up all she possessed to go bail for him. He displayed his gratitude by abandoning her immediately he regained his freedom.

BOLO'S INTEREST IN FRENCH NEWSPAPERS.

PARIS, Oct. 3.

A number of further details have become available as to the attempt of Bolo Pasha to acquire an interest in French newspapers. In only two cases is he known to have succeeded—with the *Journal*, the circumstances of which have already been explained, and with the *Rappel*, which in 1915 required new capital and accepted Bolo's offer to take a large block of shares in the paper after a searching inquiry as to his *bona fides*, which, as in the case of the *Journal*, were vouched for by the highest placed officials.

If the *Rappel* and the *Journal* were the only organs in which Bolo's money was placed, it is difficult to see how the cause of Germany has actually benefited, the former being noted for its advocacy of French annexations on the left bank of the Rhine, and the latter being the organ of the munitions campaign.

The *Figaro* to-day states that an unsuccessful attempt was made by Bolo to invest £80,000 in that newspaper in the spring of 1915, and M. Clemenceau adds in a postscript to his leading article that "the Boche also honoured me by thinking of *L'Homme Enchaîné*."

Bolo, who refused his food yesterday, has rapidly improved in health, and will this afternoon be examined by Captain Bouchardon, the military examining magistrate in charge of the case. He is reported to have declared that he would involve two important personages in his evidence.

There is considerable feeling in the country over all these scandals, and a vigorous Press argument is being conducted as to the advisability of washing dirty linen in public. One thing is clear, however, that public opinion is extremely desirous that any traitors and spies should be unearthed, tried, and punished as quickly and with as little fuss as possible.

In reference to Bolo's relations with the Marchese della Chiesa, the Pope's younger brother, and the prisoner's proposal to found a Catholic bank in Spain for peace propaganda, *La Croix* states that the scheme fell through because the Pope immediately communicated his disapproval to the Papal Nuncio in Spain. Since then the Marchese has died.

THE TIMES, MONDAY,

Oct. 1. 1917

BOLO PASHA ARRESTED.

LARGE PAYMENTS RECEIVED FROM DEUTSCHE BANK.

PARIS, Sept. 28.—As the result of important information received from the United States regarding the source of the large funds held by Bolo Pasha, a warrant for his arrest was issued this morning.

SEPTEMBER 30. The *Gaulois* states that Bolo Pasha has been lodged in the Infirmary Prison at Fresnes, the information which led to this action being a telegram from the New York police announcing the discovery of a payment of £320,000 made to him in 1916 by the Deutsche Bank.— *Reuter.*

September 30. The inquiry which led to the arrest of Bolo Pasha, who received his title from the dethroned Khedive, shows that at the beginning of the year the attention of the anti-spy service in France was directed to Bolo by reason of the frequent journeys he made in the course of the preceding years to Switzerland, Italy, and Spain. The special police then watched him, and established the fact that Bolo had just been spending in various enterprises several million francs. Bolo, when charged, energetically defended himself. He made the following declaration: "Long before the war I made investments in America, and to-day I am in possession of a fortune of several million francs, all of which is deposited in American banks. But I have never handled money either in Italy or in Switzerland."

Captain Bouchardon sent commissions of inquiry into Switzerland and the United States. In Switzerland numerous difficulties were encountered, but in the United States the authorities promised to exert themselves to the utmost to throw light on the case. Yesterday morning a telegram was addressed to the Quai D'Orsay by the United States Foreign Office, stating:

"Various sums, exceeding in all £400,000, were there deposited in the course of 1916 in the name of Paul Bolo, then staying in Paris, Rue Phalsbourg, by the Deutsche Bank, Berlin. A great part of this money has already been remitted to Paul Bolo by transfer on a French bank. Details will follow."— *Exchange Telegraph Company.*

73

BOLO EXECUTED.

1918.

THE FINAL SCENES.

(FROM OUR OWN CORRESPONDENT.)

PARIS, APRIL 17.

The sordid Bolo tragedy has ended. The condemned man was shot at 6 o'clock this morning.

At 4 o'clock there were signs of activity around the Santé Prison. By half-past 4 General Dubail, Governor of Paris, Commandant Jullien, Captain Bouchardon, Dr. Socquet, and other officials had arrived. At 5 o'clock Captain Bouchardon, Commandant Jullien, and Dr. Socquet, with the Governor of the Prison, proceeded to Bolo's cell.

Bolo was sleeping soundly, but the rattle of the lock woke him. "Oh, it's you," he said, as Commandant Jullien walked to the bedside. "I know what you've come to tell me, and I'm delighted." Bolo dressed himself with scrupulous care in a black suit and white gloves prepared for the occasion. A barber was called in to shave him and curl his moustache. When everything was ready, Bolo took out of a cigar box two white handkerchiefs, which he placed on his heart as final souvenirs for his brother and his wife.

The prisoner then received Communion at the hands of the chaplain, after which he asked for Maître Salle, his counsel, who had not arrived. A few more minutes, and a motor-car with Bolo between two gendarmes and with the chaplain was speeding through the deserted streets towards Vincennes.

No unofficial person was allowed to be present at the last scene. Bolo is reported to have walked firmly to the execution ground. He was bound to the stake, and his eyes were bandaged. The firing party consisted of 12 men.

Before leaving the prison, Captain Bouchardon is reported to have said, "Have you anything to say, Bolo?" "No," was the reply. "Have you told all?" "Don't make me say what I've not said. I merely say that I won't answer." The clerk recorded these words, and Bolo appended the signature, "Bolo Pacha."

BOLO AND BERNSTORFF.

ENSNARING THE AMBASSADOR.

OCTOBER 5.

The New York State Attorney-General has supplied the public with a dramatic sequel to the story he published yesterday concerning the activities of Bolo Pasha on behalf of Germany. The sequel occupies seven columns of newspaper print, and is a reproduction of the testimony of German-born bankers and others who assisted Bolo in his endeavour " to sink without trace" in the French Press the millions provided for him by Count Bernstorff.

" I tell you Bolo is a sly fox, a very sly fox," is the verdict on his talents given by Mr. Adolf Pavenstedt, former head of the banking house of G. Amsinck and Co. It was to Mr. Pavenstedt whom Bolo first went when he arrived in New York. He showed the German-born banker a copy of his contract with Senator Humbert and suggested to him how important it was that he should secure control of the newspaper with a circulation of 2,000,000 a day. The suggestion was accompanied by a statement that he had heard from a " friend " in Switzerland that Germany was willing to go any length to make a separate peace with France. He even outlined the terms on which, he declared, Germany could settle with France the cession of certain unspecified French Colonies to Germany in exchange for part of Alsace-Lorraine and the evacuation of the occupied parts of Northern France.

Mr. Pavenstedt informed the Attorney-General that he did not personally suppose that Bolo had any authority from Germany for these terms, but his scheme to organize sentiment for peace in the French newspapers on those lines so impressed the German banker that he hurried post haste to Washington to consult Count Bernstorff. " I must have the money, or I am a lost man," Bolo said to Mr. Pavenstedt.

Count Bernstorff found what Mr. Pavenstedt had to tell him " very interesting." The Ambassador declared that it would be of immense value if something effective could be done to change the tone of the French Press. The Ambassador promised to think the matter over. Mr. Pavenstedt returned to New York and acquainted Bolo with the fact that the German Ambassador was very interested. Bolo merely remarked, " Well, let me know what he says when he comes to New York."

A few days later M...

BOLO'S MILLIONS.

TEXT OF BERNSTORFF-JAGOW MESSAGES.

(FROM OUR CORRESPONDENT.)

NEW YORK, OCT. 7.

The text of five telegrams exchanged between Count Bernstorff and Herr von Jagow (German Foreign Secretary at the time of their dispatch) has been made public here. They run :—

NUMBER 679, Feb. 26.—I have received direct information from an entirely trustworthy source concerning a political action in one of the enemy countries which should bring peace. One of the leading political personalities of the country in question is seeking a loan of $1,700,000 (£340,000) in New York, for which security will be given. I was forbidden to give his name in writing. The affair seems to me to be of the greatest possible importance. Can the money be provided at once in New York? That the intermediary will keep the matter secret is entirely certain. I request an answer by telegram. A verbal report will follow as soon as a trustworthy person can be found to take it to Germany.—BERNSTORFF.

NUMBER 150, Feb. 29.—Answer to telegram number 679.—I agree to the loan, but only if the peace action seems to you a really serious project, as the provision of money in New York is for us at present extraordinarily difficult. If the enemy country is Russia, have nothing to do with the business, as the sum of money is too small to have any serious effect in that country. So, too, in the case of Italy, where it would not be worth while to spend so much.—JAGOW.

NUMBER 685, March 5.—Please instruct Deutsche Bank to hold nine million marks (£450,000) at the disposal of Hugo Schmidt. The affair is very promising. Further particulars follow.—BERNSTORFF.

NUMBER 692, March 20.—With reference to telegram No. 685, please advise our Minister in Berne that some one will call on him who will give him the password "Sanct Regis," and who wishes to establish relations with the Foreign Office. The intermediary further requests that influence may be brought to bear upon our Press to pass over the change in the inner political situation in France as far as possible in silence, in order that things may not be spoiled by German approval.—BERNSTORFF.

NUMBER 206, May 31.—The person announced in telegram 692 of March 20 has not yet reported himself at the Legation at Berne. Is there any more news on your side of Bolo?—JAGOW.

THE TIMES, MONDAY
OCT 1, 1917

BOLO PASHA ARRESTED.

LARGE PAYMENTS RECEIVED FROM DEUTSCHE BANK.

PARIS, Sept. 28. As the result of important information received from the United States regarding the source of the large funds held by Bolo Pasha, a warrant for his arrest was issued this morning.

SEPTEMBER 30. The *Gaulois* states that Bolo Pasha has been lodged in the Infirmary Prison at Fresnes, the information which led to this action being a telegram from the New York police announcing the discovery of a payment of £320,000 made to him in 1916 by the Deutsche Bank.— *Reuter.*

September 30. The inquiry which led to the arrest of Bolo Pasha, who received his title from the dethroned Khedive, shows that at the beginning of the year the attention of the anti-spy service in France was directed to Bolo by reason of the frequent journeys he made in the course of the preceding years to Switzerland, Italy, and Spain. The special police then watched him, and established the fact that Bolo had just been spending in various enterprises several million francs. Bolo, when charged, energetically defended himself. He made the following declaration : "Long before the war I made investments in America, and to-day I am in possession of a fortune of several million francs, all of which is deposited in American banks. But I have never handled money either in Italy or in Switzerland."

Captain Bouchardon sent commissions of inquiry into Switzerland and the United States. In Switzerland numerous difficulties were encountered, but in the United States the authorities promised to exert themselves to the utmost to throw light on the case. Yesterday morning a telegram was addressed to the Quai D'Orsay by the United States Foreign Office, stating :

"Various sums, exceeding in all £400,000, were there deposited in the course of 1916 in the name of Paul Bolo, then staying in Paris, Rue Phalsbourg, by the Deutsche Bank, Berlin. A great part of this money has already been remitted to Paul Bolo by transfer on a French bank. Details will follow."— *Exchange Telegraph Company.*

Appendix C: Newspaper Stories About *Le Bonnet Rouge*

THE TIMES, SATURDAY, SEPTEMBER 8, 1917.

"BONNET ROUGE'S" HELP TO THE ENEMY.

M. MALVY AND ALMEYREDA.

(FROM OUR OWN CORRESPONDENT.)

PARIS. SEPT. 5.

The action taken by the French authorities in the *Bonnet Rouge* case has led to the destruction of one of the enemy's strongest sources of help in this country.

A perusal of the files of that sordid sheet shows that ever since 1915 it has been busied, not only directly in the enemy interest by the advocacy of peace and through the encouragement of seditious pessimism, but also indirectly by espousing the cause of the sorry band of *embusqués*, of fraudulent Army doctors, of men such as Casement, of the liquor trade. The disguised German was its special *protégé* and Great Britain was its special enemy. It seems incredible, on reading through the articles it published—and 1,400 were obliterated by the Censor—that the clearance was not effected sooner. The *Bonnet Rouge*, though it was not one of the leviathans of the Paris Press, was nevertheless a Paris evening newspaper to be found on every kiosk of the Boulevard, and, what is perhaps more significant, it acquired its customers in the trenches. Connected with it, either through the editorial staff, the management, or by similarity of inspiration, were the *Tranchée Républicaine* and *Les Nations*, the " Primo" and the " Républicaine " news agencies. Through these channels, and through the milder medium of the *Carnet de la Semaine* and *Le Pays*, the philosophy of defeat, or at the least of Sovietism, has been preached steadily.

Reacting to the spur of M. Clemenceau, the Government have now taken action. They arrested Vigo, *alias* Almeyreda, editor-in-chief of the *Bonnet Rouge*, since mysteriously dead in prison ; Duval, and Marion, managers of the same newspaper ; and Joucla, an employee of the concern ; and the military authorities have suspended until further orders the publication of the *Bonnet Rouge*, the *Tranchée Républicaine*, and *Les Nations*. The Minister of the Interior, M. Malvy, whose duty it was to protect the country and the Army against the poison of this gang, has resigned. He could not well do otherwise of the *Bonnet Rouge*, the *Tranchée Républicaine*, and *Les Nations*. The Minister of the Interior, M. Malvy, whose duty it was to protect the country and the Army against the poison of this gang, has resigned. He could not well do otherwise. He was acquainted with Vigo, and addressed him in the familiar second person singular. He had, moreover, given him moneys from the Secret Service Fund, and of Vigo's life the most definite record is that contained in the *Gazette des Tribunaux*, which is as follows :—

" Vigo was sentenced to two months' imprisonment in 1900 for theft ; in 1901 to a year's imprisonment for the manufacture of explosives, to three years' for incitement to murder ; and in 1908 to three years' for insulting the Army ; and in 1910 he was arrested for and convicted of attempted *sabotage*.

Vigo in all this German campaign was but a puppet. He was entirely without education, and it is more than doubtful whether he was able to write the articles he signed. He has gone the way of all puppets, and lies in his grave. The articles signed by M. Badin were clever, diabolically and ironically clever, and very German. M. Badin, at any rate at some moments of his career, had his pen guided by Duval, the manager of the *Bonnet Rouge*, who now awaits his trial on the charge of having maintained " intelligence avec l'ennemi," together with four of his associates.

MALVY AND BOLO AFFAIRES.

FRANCE DEEPLY STIRRED.

M. DAUDET RETURNS TO THE CHARGE.

(FROM OUR OWN CORRESPONDENT.)

PARIS, Oct. 15.

Everything tends to show that a fresh point of crisis will shortly be reached in the development of the various *affaires* now under investigation. M. Léon Daudet has furnished the military examining magistrate, Captain Bouchardon, with all the information in his possession with regard to what he calls " the plot against France."

M. Daudet, writing in the *Action Française*, a Monarchist journal of which he is one of the political directors, says :—

Everybody has observed since the beginning of the war that there has been some rottenness somewhere which prevented Allied victory. This rottenness is the effort of German money within the countries of the Entente, and notably in France. This effort has borne upon certain individuals with certain aims, and has obtained some results. There was a German fund for the corruption of the Press. That was the Bolo fund. There was another fund to feed diplomatic intrigue—the Bülow fund—of which some ramifications already appear. There was a third fund for criminal seditious action. I will call it the Hohenlohe fund, and I know some individuals to whom the mention of this name will doubtless give a thrill . . .

This Hohenlohe fund which, according to M. Daudet is by far the most important of the three, was devoted to preparing a conspiracy, the effects of which were shown simultaneously in the Army zone and in the rear in the strikes of May and June, 1917.

I think I have proved to the examining magistrate the existence of a plot (continues M. Daudet) in which the Almeyreda gang played a most important part. I have followed step by step the conspirators in their most obscure actions and in the activities which they thought best hidden. Many witnesses will bring others to testify and it is now impossible that the truth should not be known. It is a gloomy drama in a hundred different acts which has as its centre the figures of two protagonists curiously linked together, and people of great importance. In such a drama there are a " suppliers' fund," emissaries, men and women accomplices, and a troop of players. It is like a well-regulated orchestra. I have named the leader of the orchestra to the examining magistrate.

MALVY AND BOLO AFFAIRES.

FRANCE DEEPLY STIRRED.

M. DAUDET RETURNS TO THE CHARGE.

(FROM OUR OWN CORRESPONDENT.)

PARIS, Oct. 15.

It is, therefore, with very deep interest that developments in the Malvy-Daudet matter are awaited. M. Malvy and his political friends appear to be desirous of continuing the debate upon this subject in the Chamber to-morrow. It will be remembered that it was M. Malvy himself who insisted in Parliament upon publicity being given to M. Daudet's accusation, and that before M. Daudet was examined by the judicial authority, there was a full-dress debate in Parliament upon the matter, in the course of which the chief political personages of France gave testimony on behalf of M. Malvy. The opponents of M. Malvy have, during the last few days, been waging a Press campaign against the matter again forming the subject of debate in the Chamber, arguing that the whole case has now been taken over by the judicial authorities, and that M. Malvy's reply to M. Daudet must be made, not to the Chamber of Deputies, but to the examining Magistrate who has taken M. Daudet's evidence. It seems, however, likely that to-morrow's sitting of Parliament will be devoted to M. Malvy and M. Daudet.

The Turmel and *Bonnet Rouge* cases are going on their way, and the accused in both affairs are adopting a system of defence which consists in legal obstruction, coupled with cuttle-fish tactics. M. Turmel has found no better argument of defence than to accuse a number of prominent politicians of having done the same as he has.

The publication of Bolo documents in America and rumours which reach France from Italy and England have caused a deep feeling of indignation among the general public. The conscience of the country is bitterly disgusted at the thought of the figure which France must cut abroad. It cannot be too emphatically stated that all these sinister individuals who have come to the fore during the last few months are exceptions to the general loyalty. At the Bordeaux Socialist Congress, at which delegates were present from every corner of France, I was able to assure myself of the real patriotism of the great majority of the men who certainly represent the most pacifist opinions in France.

MALVY AND BOLO AFFAIRES.

FRANCE DEEPLY STIRRED.

M. DAUDET RETURNS TO THE CHARGE.

(FROM OUR OWN CORRESPONDENT.)

PARIS, OCT. 15.

Everything tends to show that a fresh point of crisis will shortly be reached in the development of the various *affaires* now under investigation. M. Léon Daudet has furnished the military examining magistrate, Captain Bouchardon, with all the information in his possession with regard to what he calls " the plot against France."

M. Daudet, writing in the *Action Française*, a Monarchist journal of which he is one of the political directors, says :—

Everybody has observed since the beginning of the war that there has been some rottenness somewhere which prevented Allied victory. This rottenness is the effort of German money within the countries of the Entente, and notably in France. This effort has borne upon certain individuals with certain aims, and has obtained some results. There was a German fund for the corruption of the Press. That was the Bolo fund. There was another fund to feed diplomatic intrigue—the Bülow fund—of which some ramifications already appear. There was a third fund for criminal seditious action. I will call it the Hohenlohe fund, and I know some individuals to whom the mention of this name will doubtless give a thrill. . . .

This Hohenlohe fund which, according to M. Daudet is by far the most important of the three, was devoted to preparing a conspiracy, the effects of which were shown simultaneously in the Army zone and in the rear in the strikes of May and June, 1917.

I think I have proved to the examining magistrate the existence of a plot (continues M. Daudet) in which the Almeyreda gang played a most important part. I have followed step by step the conspirators in their most obscure actions and in the activities which they thought best hidden. Many witnesses will bring others to testify and it is now impossible that the truth should not be known. It is a gloomy drama in a hundred different acts which has as its centre the figures of two protagonists curiously linked together, and people of great importance. In such a drama there are a " suppliers' fund," emissaries, men and women accomplices, and a troop of players. It is like a well-regulated orchestra. I have named the leader of the orchestra to the examining magistrate.

Y, AUGUST 5, 1918.

MALVY TRIAL.

PROSECUTOR'S ADDRESS.

(FROM OUR OWN CORRESPONDENT.)

PARIS, Aug. 4.

The Public Prosecutor has finished his address in the Malvy case, and counsel for the defence is now addressing the Court.

The prosecution has abandoned altogether the charges against M. Malvy in connexion with the restitution of the famous Duval cheque, and absolves him from blame in subsidiary matters connected with the residence and permits of Russian revolutionaries and with the strikes.

Maitre Merillon dealt with all the various incidents which had been brought up in Court in which the personality of M. Caillaux appeared. Most important of these was that in which the enemy agent, Lipscher, endeavoured to bring about a peace movement with the aid of M. Caillaux. The Public Prosecutor reproached M. Malvy in this matter with having failed to do his duty, because in so doing he would have prejudiced M. Caillaux's position. Maitre Merillon added :—"The intervention of the Minister cannot be denied, and he intervened in order to save M. Caillaux, whose figure appears in every act with which I have to reproach M. Malvy."

After summing up all the facts which led to unrest in the country and to mutinies in the Army, the Public Prosecutor continued :—"These are acts of aid and assistance, and I am entitled to say that crime exists and was facilitated by the Minister." Maitre Merillon then examined "the character of this complicity," and argued that M. Malvy was unable to shelter himself behind the plea that he had ignored the objects of the activities which he assisted. The facts had been constantly brought to his notice by his officials. Maitre Merillon continued :—

M. Malvy was aware of the crime which had been committed and of the consequences which it might have. Most serious of these consequences was the execution of a large number of soldiers who had been contaminated by the propaganda which had been carried out. In June, 1917, there were ten times as many death sentences pronounced in the French Army as in any month before that date. In that one month there were as many death sentences as had been delivered during the whole year. At the present moment there are only seven death sentences a month for an army of several million men.

When she

M. MALVY'S FAREWELL.

REITERATION OF INNOCENCE.

(FROM OUR OWN CORRESPONDENT.)

PARIS, AUG. 11.

M. Malvy left Paris yesterday for the Spanish frontier. He is proceeding to San Sebastian, but it is expected that he will ultimately take up his permanent residence elsewhere in Spain.

Before his departure M. Malvy dispatched a letter to M. Deschanel, the President of the Chamber. After excusing himself to his colleagues for being necessarily absent from the next Session through his exile, the ex-Minister protests that, although acquitted of the charges of treason and complicity in treason, he had been convicted by the Senate (which, according to his advisers, is not allowed by the Constitution to make such a decision) of a new charge, not originally brought against him. He continues :—

"I have been expelled by a judgment which is at one and the same time an attack on the Constitution and the laws of the sacred right of defence. Nevertheless, desirous at this grave hour, when the fate of France is being decided, that her effort should not be weakened by any agitation, I obey the order made against me. I leave France, but I do so crying aloud that I do not and will never accept this political judgment, which turns on a question of policy."

He then states that his real crime dates from 1917, when he acted as umpire in the strikes, which he was at one time during the proceedings accused of having provoked. From this time, he says, date also the complaints against him. In the eyes of his opponents his real crime was that he had obliged the masters to meet the representatives of their employees in order to satisfy their just claims. He remains faithful " to that policy of national unity and of trust in the people, convinced that it was and remains the only policy capable of maintaining that social peace which I am happy to have been able to maintain without trouble or incident during the 42 months of my Ministry. This social peace is a condition indispensable to victory. I love my country too much to do anything to-day which could hurt her. France above everything ! "

He is going away, the ex-Minister continues, his heart bruised by injustice, but strong in the knowledge he has been wronged ; and the evidences of sympathy and democratic solidity which have been given him from all sides, and particularly from Republican and Labour organizations, have comforted his ardent faith in the triumph of justice and of the ideas for which he has suffered, and for which he is ready to suffer again. Exhorting those who may be counted his partisans, he says :—

"To all those who are with me in this cruel trial I address from the bottom of my heart a passionate appeal that they should continue to give, as before, the best of themselves for the national defence, which is more than ever inseparable from the defence of the Republic. Let the victory of France, which must be that of right and the independence of peoples, rest first in our cares. With it will sound the hour of retaliation, justice, and democracy. It is my consolation, as I put my foot into exile, to foresee both in the near future."

Appendix D: Newspaper Stories About J. Caillaux

_1918_

CAILLAUX PAPERS FROM FLORENCE.

ARRIVAL IN PARIS.

(FROM OUR CORRESPONDENT.)

PARIS, JAN. 18.

The documents and securities seized in M. Caillaux's safe at the Banca di Sconto, Florence, arrived in Paris this morning in charge of three Italian magistrates.

M. Herbette, Director of the Ministry for Foreign Affairs, Major Pottier, representing General Dubail, Military Governor of Paris, and M. Priolet were on the platform to receive the trunk, which was immediately taken to the room of Captain Bouchardon, the Examining Magistrate, at the Palais de Justice, by two detective-inspectors. This afternoon the seals will be broken in the presence of M. Caillaux and Italian officials, and an inventory will be drawn up.

The Unified Socialist Group, on the motion of M. Renaudel, has unanimously voted the following order of the day :—

The Socialist Group, anxious to assure the good administration of justice, recalling also the undertaking given by the Ministry for Foreign Affairs under the last Government to publish under its responsibility translations of documents of a diplomatic character ; regretting that this general measure has not been applied specially and at the outset, to documents such as the so-called "American" dispatches, which are to serve to enlighten not only justice, but also public opinion ; noting that the consequence of this omission has been to place public opinion in the face of three different arguments ; expects the Government itself to furnish exact details of the documents found at Florence.

Among the witnesses to be called by Bolo, whose trial before the Third Court-martial begins on February 4, are the ex-Khedive, Sadik Pasha ; Herr Meyer, of Hamburg, banker ; Herr Pavenstedt, United States agent of the Hamburg Bank, and various other enemy subjects. On this fantastic list figure also the names of M. Caillaux and a few Deputies.

M. CAILLAUX'S FLORENCE SAFE.

A ROME CONVERSATION.

(FROM OUR CORRESPONDENT.)

PARIS, JAN. 21.

All formalities in regard to the handing over of the contents of M. Caillaux's Florence safe to Captain Bouchardon, the Examining Magistrate, will be completed to-day. Before returning to Italy Colonel Chiapirone, who is Chief of the Rome Military Tribunal, with jurisdiction over the whole of Italy, will—probably this afternoon—give evidence before Captain Bouchardon as a witness concerning M. Caillaux's visits to Italy and Cavallini's doings there and in Paris.

M. de Maizière, special representative of the _Petit Parisien_ in Rome, reveals a conversation which he had with M. Caillaux when the latter and his wife were staying at the Hôtel de Russie in December, 1916, as M. and Mme. Reynouard.

M. Maizière told M. Caillaux that his reputation in Rome was very bad, and that the French Embassy was very severe in its judgment of his attitude. M. Caillaux flew into a passion, and protested that there was no better Frenchman than himself. "If," he said, "the men governing us are sure of success, if they give us victory, they will have no sincerer partisan than myself, no more humble admirer." To give weight to his words he knocked over a flower-pot. Then, picking it up, he continued :—"But if those men fail woe betide them, woe betide Briand," and brought down his list on the flowerstand. M. Caillaux accompanied M. de Maizière to the door, and on the way he remarked that he was about to begin an action against _The Times_, which had insulted him. He was sure to win the case, he declared. M. de Maizière adds that M. Caillaux appeared to be verging on madness. It would have been useless to report the conversation at that time, as the Censor would not have passed it, but now M. de Maizière has been requested to give evidence before the Examining Magistrate on the subject.

85

CAILLAUX TRIAL FIXED.

(FROM OUR OWN CORRESPONDENT.)

PARIS, OCT. 15.

The Council of Ministers met this morning and decided the terms of the Decree arraigning M. Caillaux before the High Court of Justice of the Senate, together with MM. Loustalot and Comby. The Decree fixes Tuesday, October 29, as the date of convocation of the Senate.

At the front the measures which had to be taken included the change of every Army Command and Staff. In the interior of the country he contemplated dismissing the Chamber, and mentioned certain regiments which he intended to bring to Paris. He also proposed the arrest and prosecution of the direct and indirect authors of the war.

The "Rubicon" was, however, his great instrument of government. By this special measure legislation by decree replaced the usual constitutional government. Among his possible collaborators figure the names of Landau, who is now undergoing penal servitude, and Almeyreda, the late editor of the *Bonnet Rouge*. M. Ceccaldi was to be appointed Prefect of Police—a slightly more exalted post than that which he occupies to-day as M. Caillaux's counsel. When once the Chamber had voted peace, the "Rubicon" was going to be "imposed" upon the nation. He intended, moreover, to get control of the *Matin* and the *Journal*, and to utilize in this connexion the services of the criminal Almeyreda.

The indictment mentions that certain documents of German origin had been discovered, dealing with the Agadir period, which throw a singular and disturbing light upon M. Caillaux's attitude towards Germany, and it suggests that M. Calmette's knowledge of these documents may not have been altogether foreign to M. Calmette's assassination by Mme. Caillaux.

M. Lescouvé then examines the activities of M. Caillaux during his mission to South America, where through a German-Italian named Minotto, who at the outbreak of war was employed by the Deutsche Bank in London, he would appear to have entertained indirect relations with Count Luxburg, the German Minister famous through his "Spurlos versenkt."

CAILLAUX TRIAL FIXED.

DEFEATIST ACTIVITIES.

RELATIONS WITH ENEMY AGENTS.

(FROM OUR OWN CORRESPONDENT.)

PARIS, Oct. 29.

The Senate sat again to-day as a High Court to hear read the indictment against M. Caillaux, which is based on a *dossier* of over 7,000 documents. M. Caillaux was not present.

At the outset of the indictment the Public Prosecutor, M. Lescouvé, recalled the circumstances which brought about the prosecution of M. Caillaux, those of the defeatist journals—the *Bonnet Rouge* of Almeyreda, the *Tranchée Républicaine* of Landau—and of the Cavallini, Lenoir, and Desouche scandals. The Prosecutor continued :—

With regard to the war policy of M. Caillaux, who posed as a party chief and future Prime Minister, the Examining Judge (Captain Bouchardon) was able to lay his hand upon two series of documents which had been placed for security in the Florence safe in November, 1916, and which can leave no doubt of the state of mind of the accused person. In an anonymous memorandum entitled " Les responsables—la guerre et la paix," which is composed of two manuscript copies entirely in M. Caillaux's handwriting, one of which was a mere first attempt, dated April 6, 1915, and three typewritten copies of the actual text, the accused endeavours to show, with an ingenuity worthy of a better cause, that if Germany willed the war, and even declared it, she, as a matter of fact, only willed it hesitatingly. However improbable this may appear, for M. Caillaux those responsible for the war were not so much Germany and her leaders as the French Press and the French Government.

Together with this memorandum were also found in the Florence safe a political note in which M. Caillaux outlined the steps to be taken, when he assumed power as Prime Minister, in order to make peace [the " Rubicon " document]. M. Caillaux's programme, while it was one of immediate peace

Le Président de la Commission sénatoriale des finances est né au Mans, le 30 mars 1863. Technicien des questions financières et homme d'État il est le fils d'Eugène-Alexandre Caillaux, ingénieur et homme d'État, qui vécut de 1822 à 1896,

JOSEPH CAILLAUX

Sénateur
2, Square de l'Av. du Bois, Paris.
et à Mamers. (Sarthe)

fut aussi député de la Sarthe à l'Assemblée Nationale, sénateur de 1876 à 1882 et qui détint les portefeuilles des Travaux publics et des Finances.

M. Joseph Caillaux a appartenu pendant dix ans à ce corps des inspecteurs des Finances, dont l'accès a toujours été réservé aux techniciens d'élite et qui ouvre, l'administration quittée, des carrières privées non moins brillantes, notamment les conseils des établissements de crédit. Mais pour lui, grand bourgeois français, la recherche désintéressée du pouvoir a primé toute autre préoccupation. Ses compatriotes sarthois l'envoient à la Chambre en 1898. Sa compétence financière est connue. Il appartient, après un bref stage au cours duquel il s'initie mieux aux finesses de la vie parlementaire, aux ministères Waldeck-Rousseau (1899-1902), Clemenceau (1906-1909) et Monis (1911). Progressiste à son entrée au Parlement, il évolue vers le parti radical qu'il sera appelé à présider. A la chute du cabinet Monis, il prend. — nous sommes en 1911 — la présidence du Conseil et le portefeuille de l'Intérieur ; c'est lui qui, en 1907-1909, avait défendu et obtenu la création de l'impôt sur le revenu, c'est lui qui — plus tard — s'opposera à l'impôt sur le capital qu'il combattra. Mais, en 1911, l'avenir est sombre. Nos vues sur le protectorat marocain ne sont pas sans porter ombrage à l'Allemagne et le Président du Conseil se trouve subitement devant la pire des difficultés diplomatiques, qui depuis Fachoda et avant 1914, ait fait passer des nuits blanches à un chef de gouvernement français. Par manière de chantage, l'empereur Guillaume II envoie un beau jour un navire de guerre à Agadir... et nous sommes forcés de négocier. Quels reproches n'adressera-t-on pas à ce ministre pacifique et réaliste pour avoir réussi à nous assurer la prépondérance au Maroc et pour avoir échangé la reconnaissance tacite de notre protectorat contre un territoire congolais ! Depuis cette époque troublée, tant de sang a été versé, tant d'angoisses ont été ressenties qu'on s'explique mal aujourd'hui la résistance du ministre de Selves acceptant, enfin, avec un mauvais gré qui devait aller jusqu'à sa démission, la convention allemande que la Chambre avait ratifiée à une imposante majorité, en décembre 1911. M. Joseph Caillaux abandonne le pouvoir le 11 janvier 1912. Il entre, en 1913, dans la combinaison Doumergue, qu'il quitte le 10 mars 1914 à la suite des dramatiques événements que l'on connaît. Pendant la guerre, le gouvernement utilise sa compétence et son autorité. De 1914 à 1915, il est investi de missions dans l'Amérique du Sud. A nul endroit, M. Joseph Caillaux ne cache son opinion. Il est partisan d'une paix rapide et

3. FRENCH SECRET SERVICE.—The story of the French secret service during the war contains many sad chapters. It was often unfortunate in the choice of some of its agents, as in the case of a woman who revealed to the Germans the entire French espionage system in Belgium, thereby causing the arrest of some eighty persons. As it is impossible to reconstitute a secret service system in a foreign country when a war is in progress, France after the catastrophe in Belgium was forced to depend on the British intelligence department for information about the enemy. But from the first the French secret service was hampered by Louis J Malvy, minister of the interior, who in spite of attacks and exposures held office in six cabinets from March 18, 1914, until August 31, 1917, when he was forced to resign. He was subsequently tried and sentenced to five years' banishment, and the payment of a small fine, but retained his civil rights. Malvy represented the Radical Socialists and their former chief, Joseph Caillaux, the ex-premier, was also accused of having had dealings with the Germans. Until his resignation in 1917, Malvy was retained in office by different premiers through their fear of a Socialist uprising, which would have upset the government. The story of his dealings with the foes of the republic without and within is a long one. He permitted dangerous enemy agents to remain in France and continue their work; he furnished passports to French traitors which enabled them to visit German agents in Switzerland; he was hand in glove with the "Defeatists" [see FRANCE: 1918], and with the gang connected with the *Bonnet Rouge* publication whose head, the notorious anarchist Almereyda, committed suicide, or was murdered in prison, while the editor Duval was executed and six associates received prison sentences at hard labor for terms of from two to ten years. It was proved at Malvy's trial that the Apache editor of the *Bonnet Rouge* was a constant visitor at the ministry of the interior and that Almereyda forced Malvy to liberate great numbers of agitators, anarchists, and all-around criminals. The Second Bureau consisting of army police which tried to arrest enemy agents and traitors was finally suppressed through Malvy's efforts. Considering the great number of enemies behind the front in France who were left free to work their will, we can only marvel that the national defense remained integrally sound until the end of the war.—Based on E. Everitt, *British secret service during the Great War;* S. T. Felstead, *German spies at bay;* E. Hough *The web;* F. Strothers, *Fighting Germany's spies.*—See also below: III. Press reports and censorship: d.

4. AMERICAN INTELLIGENCE SERVICE.—"Though a fairly careful perusal of the files of 'M. I. D.,' as the Division of Military Intelligence is commonly referred to in the army, discloses no evidence that German spies of the caliber of Karl Lody and Bolo Pasha operated in this country during the war, they do contain the *dossiers* of enemy agents whose personalities and exploits meet all the requirements for characters in spy fiction. Probably the nearest approach to the high-class spy, as made familiar by the articles in the Sunday supplements and the magazines, was Captain Franz von Rintelen. . . . The other enemy agents who operated in this country were, for the most part, former privates in the German Army or petty officers and stewards on German liners, the most picturesque of the lot, a man named Bode, being so inefficient that he was dismissed by his own government, whereupon, being without funds, he surrendered himself to the American authorities. . . . Let it be perfectly clear, however, that nothing is further from my intention than to minimize the deadly gravity of the German spy menace in this country during the war, or to suggest that, had no steps been taken to check it, it would not have caused the loss of millions of American dollars and thousands of American lives. That the national safety was not more gravely imperilled by these enemy agents was not due to their inefficiency, or to the weakness of the German espionage system, but to the efficiency, resourcefulness, and unremitting vigilance of the Division of Military Intelligence. . . . Though military intelligence work was undertaken by the army in 1885, in response to a demand for information from the Secretary of War, it was not until the United States found itself an actual belligerent in the Great War that the immense importance of the work was fully realized. Incredible as it may seem, when General Pershing set sail for France in the spring of 1917, the entire personnel of the Military Intelligence Section, as it was then called, consisted of four officers . . . and three clerks. Due, however, to the forcible arguments and the breadth of vision of its first chief, Colonel Ralph H. Van Deman, the foundation was laid for the present vast organization, whose activities expanded, at the demands of war, until, when the Armistice was signed, they virtually

Appendix E: Newspaper Stories About J. Minotto

NAMES CAILLAUX IN PLOT TO SPLIT ALLIES IN NEW WAR

Count James Minotto Confesses, Revealing Intrigue with Luxburg in Buenos Aires.

HE WAS THE GO-BETWEEN

Swift's Son-in law Says France, Italy, and Spain Were to Join the Teutons.

AGAINST BRITAIN AND RUSSIA

Confession Made Here to Deputy Attorney General Becker as Agent of French Republic.

Count James Minotto, the German nobleman who is a son-in-law of Louis F. Swift, the Chicago packer, and who, according to Secretary of the Navy Josephus Daniels, tried to get a place in the Naval Intelligence Service of this country, has made a startling confession to the American authorities regarding a plot engaged in by Joseph I. Caillaux, the former French Premier, Count Luxburg, former German Minister to the Argentine, and himself, to disrupt the Entente Alliance and to bring about a new war, in which the Teutonic powers, France, Italy, and Spain would be arrayed against Great Britain and Russia. The full report of the Minotto confession is now on the way to the French authorities in Paris.

Swifts Came to His Aid.

Minotto, Seebeck, and Kuhn were all arrested as a result of the Minotto inquiry. The last two were promptly ordered interned. Minotto was arrested and his wife's family immediately came to his assistance, and a long and bitter fight was started, the object of which was to keep the German out of the internment camp. Minotto was released under $50,000 bail, his bondsman being Louis F. Swift, his father-in-law.

After his arrest Minotto continued to maintain that he was Italian and not German. His father, Count Demetrius Minotto, be put forward as a member of

Minotto, whose internment as an enemy alien was fought by his wife's family, who maintained that the Count was an Italian and an ally of the United States, was brought to New York last week from the internment prison near Fort Oglethorpe, Ga. He was taken before Deputy Attorney General Alfred L. Becker, who represented the French Government and the Federal authorities. At first, Minotto was not inclined to talk, but he finally told the story in all its details.

The Countess Minotto, mother of Count James, was, before her marriage, the famous German actress Agnes Sorma. Mme. Sorma will be remembered by old theatregoers as the star in Hauptmann's "Sunken Bell," which was played in German at the Irving Place Theatre some twenty years ago. The Countess and her husband are both in the United States at present. They went to Chicago last November to aid their son when he was fighting against the Government's order of internment.

Mr. Becker said last night that for the present he was not in a position to make public the full details of the confession made by Minotto. The story when told in full, he said, would be one of the most remarkable in the history of international intrigue and would show up Caillaux as a plotter compared to whom Bolo Pacha was a mere novice. Bolo sought to corrupt French public opinion through the publication of a few newspapers. Caillaux on the other hand, sought to betray not only his own but two other nations as well, one of them Italy, an ally of France, and the other Spain, a friend of France. Had the plot succeeded, it was pointed

The New York Times
Published: October 29, 1918
Copyright © The New York Times

COUNTESS MINOTTO AT HOME.

Count's Father-in-law, Louis F. Swift, Refuses Comment.

Special to The New York Times.

CHICAGO, Oct. 28.—The Countess Minotto, formerly Miss Ida May Swift, is living at the home of her father in Lake Forest. Minotte's father, Count Demetrio Minotto, and his wife, formerly Agnes Sorma, a German actress, spent the summer at Glencoe.

Louis F. Swift was at his Lake Forest house tonight. When asked if he could throw any light on the Count's statement in the Caillaux-Luxburg matter, he said: "I haven't heard one word about it. I know nothing about it. I have no comment to make."

SWIFT'S SON-IN-LAW MAY BE INTERNED

Presidential Warrant Issued for Count James Minotto as an Alien Enemy.

IS OUT ON $100,000 BAIL

His Efforts to Enter Naval Intelligence Bureau Led to Internment of Two German Associates.

Special to The New York Times.

WASHINGTON, May 13.—Attorney General Gregory today authorized the issuance of a Presidential warrant for and the internment of Count James Minotto, under the President's proclamation relating to the internment of alien enemies.

Count Minotto is a son-in-law of Louis F. Swift, the Chicago meat packer, and has been under investigation by the Federal authorities since prior to last October, when he was arrested on the technical accusation that he was liable to become a charge when he entered this country. He has been under consideration by the Navy Department, the Department of Labor, and the Department of Justice.

In March the Department of Justice refused to deport him on the charges preferred by the Director of Naval Intelligence because of suspicions aroused by his German birth and associations, but dismissal of the arrest warrant was postponed until the Department of Justice should decide whether the Count could be interned as an enemy alien. Pending action by the Attorney General Count Minotto was permitted to remain at liberty on $50,000 bail furnished by his father-in-law.

Count Minotto is the man whose efforts to obtain a position in the Naval Intelligence Bureau led to the arrest of his associates, George von Seebeck and Fritz Kuhn in New York, and their internment as enemy aliens. Minotto came to the United States in 1914, arriving on the Campania on Aug. 22 in company with Kuhn and von Seebeck. Before his arrival here he was a representative of one of the largest German banks in London. His father claimed Italian parentage, his mother was a German. Count Minotto spent most of his life in Germany.

Soon after arriving in this country Count Minotto obtained employment with the Guaranty Trust Company of New York, and was sent by that company twice to South America.

Special to The New York Times.

CHICAGO, May 13.—Count James Minotto, son-in-law of Louis F. Swift, Chicago packer, who recently won his fight against deportation as an enemy alien, was arrested today on a Presidential warrant. He is still held under $50,000

BLUE DEVILS AT CAPITAL

Received by President and Entertained on One-Day Visit.

Special to The New York Times.

WASHINGTON, May 13.—President Wilson, the French Ambassador and Mme. Jusserand, the Washington Red Cross, and French residents of the capital today paid honor to the "Blue Devils" of France, who made a one-day visit here as guests of the Government. Each of the ninety visitors wore a War Cross.

President Wilson received the visitors in morning and this afternoon the French High Commissioner, M. André Tardieu, gave a reception in their honor at the New Willard with the French Ambassador and Mme. Jusserand to assist in receiving. M. Tardieu made a short speech of introduction, to which the Ambassador replied. Both speakers dwelt on the great work accomplished by France, congratulating this particular band of participants, and welcoming them to the United States, where much is hoped for from their example. A sight-seeing tour by motor and a luncheon with attentions from the Red Cross

CAILLAUX IN COURT; SPIRIT UNBROKEN

Called as Witness in Bonnet Rouge Affair, He Seeks to Plead His Own Case.

ENTERS LIKE A DICTATOR

Ex-Premier, Kept to the Issue, Says He Never Heard of Banker Marx Till July, 1917.

Copyright, 1918, by The New York Times Company
Special Cable to THE NEW YORK TIMES.

PARIS, May 11.—For the first time since his arrest over two months ago on charges of treason, Paris saw today ex-Premier Joseph Caillaux, who for several years was undoubtedly the most powerful and, in the opinion of many, the most dangerous public man in France, whether in or out of office, make his appearance in public. He was called as a witness in the Bonnet Rouge trial.

Caillaux entered the room in which the court-martial sat with his head high and lacking not a jot of the characteristic arrogance and pride which led him to claim the right to be the dictator of his country's fate and which brought him to his present position. The prisoner is awaiting trial by a military court on the gravest charges that can be laid against a politician. His evidence was unimportant in itself and the whole interest in his appearance was purely personal.

It was evident from the man's whole manner that confinement in a prison cell and the long investigation he has undergone have not in the slightest degree diminished his fighting power. He marched in surrounded by armed guards with the air of a dictator in the midst of his escort of honor. His answers were given with complete assurance and a steady gaze at the President of the court-martial which marked him as a man entirely without fear, who was prepared to fight to the end. With all the personal force with which he has often faced and quelled an antagonistic chamber he attempted more than once to get outside the narrow limits of the question on which he had been called with a view to express for the benefit of the greater audience in the country at large some part of his own defence against the charges of treason, and it was only the firmness of the President of the court-martial which kept him from making use of the court as a personal platform.

Caillaux's ---

Bibliography

Alfred Cobban, *A History of Modern France* (Harmondsworth, England: Penguin Books, 1961)

H.C. Engelbrecht and F.C. Hanighen, *Merchants of Death: A Study of the International Armaments Industry* (New York: Dodd, Mead & Co., 1934)

Robert H. Ferrell, *Woodrow Wilson and World War I, 1917-1921* (New York: Harper & Row, 1985)

Julian Green, *Memories of Happy Days* (New York: Harper, 1942)

Francis W. Halsey, *The Literary Digest History of the World War* (New York: Funk & Wagnall, 1919-1920)

Russell W. Howe, *Mata Hari, The True Story* (New York: Dodd, Mead & Co., 1986)

Tibor Koeves, *Satan in Top Hat: The Biography of Franz von Papen* (New York: Alliance Book Corp., 1941)

Henry Landau, *The Enemy Within: The Inside Story of German Sabotage in America* (New York: G.P. Putnam's Sons, 1937)

Joseph Nelson Larned, *The New Larned History, Vol. 9-12* (Springfield, MA: C.A. Nichols Publishing Co., 1922)

Robert Lajeunesse and Robert Vorms, Les Editions Lajeunesse. (Paris: 1936)

Emmet J. Scott, *Official History of the American Negro in the World War* (New York: Arno Press, 1969)

W. A. Swanbert, *Citizen Hearst: A Biography of William Randolph Hearst* (New York: Scribner, 1961)

Barbara Tuchman, *The Guns of August* (London: Four Square, 1964)

Barbara Tuchman, *The Zimmerman Telegram* (London: Constable, 1959)

Ernest Vizetelly, *Republican France, 1870-1912* (Boston: Small, Maynard & Co., 1913)

John K. Winkler, *William Randolph Hearst, A New Appraisal* (New York: Hastings House, 1955)

Leon Wolff, *In Flanders Field: The 1917 Campaign* (London: Longmans, 1959)

ALSO:

National Archives, Washington, DC (1914-1920)

Depositions of A. Pavenstedt and others, taken by the Attorney General of New York for use in the Bolo trial. National Archives, 1914-1920.

Dictionnaire National Des Contemporains (Paris: 1964)

The Times [London} 1900-1920

The New York Times 1914-1920

The Chicago Daily Tribune 1917-1920

Index

J

Jusserand, J.J. (French Ambassador to U.S.) 31, 33

K

Kameneff 25
Kolontai 25
Koslovsky 25
Kuhn, Fritz 39

L

Labori, Maitre 2
Lenin 25
Lenoir, Pierre 32, 37, 38
Lescouve, General 37, 40
Leymarie, Jean 29
Lipscher, Count 37
LuxBurg, Count 8, 37, 38, 41

M

Malvy, Louis-Jean 27, 43
Maunoury (Prefect of Police) 28
McAdoo, William Gibbs 39
McCahill, Frank 18
Mercain 25
Minotto, James 8, 39, 43
Morgan, Harjes & Co. 24
Morgan, J.P. & Co. 13, 17, 18, 23, 24, 31
Morgan, J.P. (John Pierpont), Jr. 17, 18
Morgan, J.S. & Co. 17
Morgan, Junius S. 17
Mornet, Andre 28, 37, 43

N

National Archives - File #117993 49
Neill, C.E. 22
Nivelle, Robert N. 25

O

Ouff, Sonia 24

P

Pavenstedt, Adolph 21, 22, 23, 24, 32, 96
Poincare, Raymond 2, 6, 7, 11, 34

R

"Responsables, Les-La Guece Et La Paix" 40
Reynouard, Henriette (Madame Caillaux) 37
Royal Bank of Canada 22, 23, 24
"Rubicon" 40

S

Sadik Pacha 13, 15
Sallie, Albert 33, 41
Schmidt, Hugo 23, 32, 33
Sivers 25
Socquet, Dr. 34
Sumenson 25
Swift, Ida May 39
Swift, Louis 39, 43

T

Tisza, Count 38
Trotsky, Leon 11, 25

U

U.S. Steel 24

V

Van Anda, C.V. 24
Viviani (Minister of Defense) 38
Von Hintze, Rear Admiral 17
Von Jagow, Gottlieb 15, 22
Von Papen, Franz 17
Von Schoen, Baron 11
Von Zebeck, Count 39
Voyer, Colonel 32, 33, 34

W

Wilson, Woodrow 17, 95

Y

Yeghen, Mahmud Pacha 15

Z

Zinovieff 25